"Walt Disney, who had demanding standards, would go for Jim Cathcart's comprehensive new book, *The Acorn Principle*. Walt told me the story about fulfillment that you'll discover in the book. You will find the Fulfillment Grid outstanding!"

—Mike Vance,
speaker and chairperson of Creative Thinking Association
and author of *Think Out of the Box* and *Break Out of the Box*

"Jim Cathcart is one of the brightest, dearest, and most comprehensive speakers I know. In this powerful book he will help you discover and express your true self, accelerate your success, and improve your quality of life."

—Jack Canfield,
coauthor of the *New York Times* best-seller *Chicken Soup for the Soul*
and *The Aladdin Factor*

"Jim Cathcart has lived a life only dreamed of by most people. He not only practices in his life what he teaches, in this book he reveals how you can fulfill your dreams. Take *The Acorn Principle* home; follow its prescriptions; with Jim at your side, find out how rich, full, and rewarding your life can be."

—Dr. Blaine N. Lee,
author of *The Power Principle: Influence with Honor*
and vice president of Franklin Covey Company

"A well-written, pragmatic, thoughtful, and inspirational guide to discovering who we are, what we can become, and the search for meaning in the journey."

—Warren Farrell, Ph.D.,
author of *Why Men Are the Way They Are* and *The Myth of Male Power*

"Forget any other book you have ever read on personal growth, success, or achievement. Jim Cathcart has set the new standard. *The Acorn Principle* is, simply, the best book ever . . . the most complete, practical, and usable self-improvement book I've ever read. It is destined to dwarf all the rest for all time!"

—Bill Brooks,
author of *Niche Selling, High Impact Selling,*
and *You're Working Too Hard to Make the Sale*

"Jim's acorn-oak metaphor is inspired! To realize that we already have all we need to make our lives work is an idea so powerful as to defy description. So donate all your self-help books to the next church sale. This intellectual and spiritual feast is all you'll need to be the you that you have always been."

—Bill Grove,
first president of the National Speakers Association,
Toastmasters International Golden Gavel Winner,
and FSA Lifetime Achievement Award

"Jim Cathcart is a master, but he'll never brag about it. If you meet him today, you'll find one of the classiest, fulfilling people on earth. Twenty years ago, Jim was a government bureaucrat and weighed two hundred pounds. What happened in between was Jim's own growth process, which he outlines in *The Acorn Principle*. The seeds of greatness were always there—they just needed nourishing. This book gives you the simple steps to finding your mission—and developing your own mastery of life. Jim says he wants to have a positive influence on mankind—*The Acorn Principle* promises to have that impact."

—Peter Meisen,
president of Global Energy Network Institute

"The best example of how sound a principle is, is to live it. . . . Jim Cathcart does! I've met and worked with Jim, and to see how he has internalized *The Acorn Principle,* enthusiastically applies it, and is quite the success story, is proof enough for me!"

—James T. Brown,
Fox Sports

"*The Acorn Principle* guides us on a fascinating journey within! If we all mastered the techniques described within this book to more fully and completely know ourselves, and we adopted the empowering and life-enhancing skills Jim teaches, we could live our lives with more purpose and direction, and with an enormous amount of joy and freedom!"

—Les Brown,
motivational speaker and author of
Live Your Dreams and *It's Not Over Till You Win*

"*The Acorn Principle* is a metaphor of profound power and exceptional usefulness. Jim Cathcart has that rare ability to explain complex concepts clearly, without over-simplifying them. This book has helped me to transcend limitations I didn't even know I had!"

—Gregory J. P. Godek,
author of the best-sellers *1001 Ways to Be Romantic*
and *Love—The Course They Forgot to Teach You in School*

"This book is wonderful! It explains perhaps the most important single principle you can ever learn to guarantee success, happiness, and lifelong prosperity."

—Brian Tracy,
international speaker and author of *Maximum Achievement*

"*The Acorn Principle* brings a new perspective to self-improvement: success and happiness do not come from changing yourself, but rather from discovering your natural talents and aligning your life accordingly. In reading this book, you will discover seven systems that exist within you. These systems make up your 'Acorn Profile.' With the knowledge of these 'seeds,' you can transcend your perceived limitations and expand your imagined possibilities."

—Bettie B. Youngs, Ph.D.,
author of *Taste-Berry Tales* and *Gifts of The Heart*

"*The Acorn Principle* is a masterful journey of self-discovery. It is one of those rare books that beckon you not just to read it cover to cover but over and over. Jim Cathcart has given us a road map to achieve our greatest potential. Thank you, Jim!"

—Tony Alessandra, Ph.D.,
author of *Charisma* and *The Platinum Rule*

"This is a fabulous book! It will help you to unveil new insights in your personal life and chart a winning course in your professional life. Read it to be inspired. Study it to be informed. Live it to be happy."

—Nido R. Qubein,
author of *How to Be a Great Communicator* and *Stairway to Success*,
chairman and CEO of Creative Services, Inc., and past president
of the National Speakers Association

"We have entered a new era wherein human knowledge and skills are more important than ever. As technology allows us to connect with each other in new and powerful ways, the human quality of those connections becomes critical. *The Acorn Principle* provides a powerful guide to a lifelong process of self-exploration and discovery, allowing readers to maximize their true potential and connect with others as never before."

—Daniel Burrus,
leading technology forecaster and author of *Technotrends*

"Jim Cathcart is one of the smartest and most successful people I know. He walks his talk in business and in his personal life. *The Acorn Principle* is the synthesis of Jim's twenty-plus years in the field of self-help, during which time he has been an outstanding leader and innovator. I urge you to read, digest, and embrace what he offers."

—Jeff Davidson,
author of *The Joy of Simple Living*

"The tiny acorn for successful living lies within all of us. Jim Cathcart not only *illustrates* how to nurture it into full bloom—he *demonstrates* how in his own remarkable life."

—Bruce Belland,
founder of The Four Preps and syndicated/radio host
of *Pop Americana*

"Books on self-actualization have for decades talked about the importance of 'knowing yourself,' 'self-discovery,' and how that discovery can lead to greater personal, spiritual, and professional success. Jim Cathcart has finally and effectively told us how to navigate this journey of self-awareness. Calling upon his twenty years as a professional communicator, he undertakes, and achieves, the daunting task of making a complex subject palatable, readable, and most important, achievable.

"Complete with concrete examples, exercises, and carefully researched models, Jim gently but firmly helps the reader discover the psychological, spiritual, and even cultural seeds that make each of us who we are. He then demonstrates how to walk the delicate balance between accepting what we must and changing what we can, all with an eye on growth, peace of mind, and internal and external achievement."

—Sondra Thiederman, Ph.D.,
author of *Profiting in America's Multicultural Marketplace*
and *Bridging Cultural Barriers for Corporate Success*

"Jim Cathcart is not only one of America's most effective speakers, he is a great writer who shares a meaningful message on personal development, growth, and leadership in this great [book], *The Acorn Principle* . . . a true leadership handbook!"

—Ed Foreman,
former United States Congressman (Texas and New Mexico),
author, speaker, and entrepreneur

"The beauty of Cathcart's teachings in *The Acorn Principle* is his directness—his honesty and heart. We quickly learn that personal growth, success, and fulfillment come from *uncovering* our uniqueness, from *discovering* our true talents. It's a process of discerning *natural fit*. Be an acorn! Grow and develop! Rejoice in yourself!"

—Jim Tunney, Ed.D.,
coauthor of *Chicken Soup for the Sports Fan's Soul*

"Jim Cathcart has gone to the very heart of the issues that we face in this country, that being our Values. There could not be a better source of information at a better time than what Jim Cathcart has to offer. This is a must-read, listen, understand topic for the twenty-first century."

—Sheila Murray Bethel,
best-selling author of *Making a Difference*

"Jim Cathcart has managed to squeeze one of the great truths of life into a tiny little acorn-size symbol that you can't forget. He's incredibly talented at distilling major life lessons down to parables that stick with you. I think of his 'acorn principle' every week and find it powerfully beneficial in my personal and professional relationships. Just this week, I avoided a potentially harmful encounter with my assistant by reflecting on Jim's teachings. I've used them with great benefit as I parent my daughter, too. Jim, himself, is an authentic, genuine reflection of the principles he espouses. I've never met a finer person or an author with more power to change lives for the better."

—George R. Walther,
author of *Power Talking*

"Very thought provoking—a different, refreshing approach."

—Barbara Hanson,
Thomas Publishing Company

"*The Acorn Principle* is an intellectually elegant, concise program that makes you reach deep inside yourself to develop your full potential for a fulfilling life."

—Rob Sommer,
television producer and creator of *Speaking of Success* series

"*The Acorn Principle* approaches the complexities of business in a simple, effective way. Nowadays simplicity is golden—a key factor in crunching time. This [book] explores the intelligence of practicality."

—Doc Lew Childre,
Institute for Heart Math

"Thought provoking and stimulating, yet straightforward and easy to understand. Practical. Clearly applicable to 'real life'."

—Annie Morrisey,
educational services director of Working Solutions, Inc.

"I've never seen a book that has conveyed so much useful information. With pen and paper handy, you need to read *The Acorn Principle* over and over and over. You will be richly rewarded for doing so."

—Vince Lombardi, Jr.

The
Acorn Principle

Also by Jim Cathcart

Inspiring Others to Win
The Professional Speaker Business System (audio)
The Sales Professional's Idea-a-Day Guide
The Winning Spirit
Speaking Secrets of the Masters
The Acorn Principle (audio)
Rethinking Yourself (video)
Be Your Own Sales Manager
Relationship Selling
Insights into Excellence
Selling by Objectives
Win Through Relationships (video)
Think Service (video)
Meeting with Success (audio)
Helping People Grow (video)
SuperStar Selling (audio)
The Business of Selling
Relationship Strategies (audio)
Communication Dynamics

The Acorn Principle

Know Yourself —Grow Yourself

Discover, Explore, and Grow
the Seeds of Your Greatest Potential

Jim Cathcart

Foreword by Denis E. Waitley, Ph.D.

St. Martin's Press ❧ New York

Design by Diane Hobbing of Snap-Haus Graphics

Library of Congress Cataloging-in-Publication Data

Cathcart, Jim.
    The acorn principle : know yourself—grow yourself / Jim Cathcart.
        p.   cm.
    Includes bibliographical references.
    ISBN 0-312-19652-0
    1. Life skills.   I. Title.
HQ2037.C38   1998
646.7—dc21   98-21123
                                                          CIP

First Edition: September 1998
10 9 8 7 6 5 4 3 2 1

Contents

Acknowledgments

When I celebrated the ten-year anniversary of my business way back in 1987, I asked the question, "Whom should I take time to thank?" The ensuing celebration was focused on them instead of me. I don't recall ever having more fun. That's a great question for all of us to ask whenever we reach a milestone. The fact that we made it this far is proof that many other people have contributed to our advancement. This book is certainly no exception.

Now I am beyond the twentieth anniversary of Cathcart Institute and have even more people to thank. Many people have molded my thinking and shaped this book, some through direct personal involvement with this project, others through their personal interaction with me. In 1973, Harold Gash, a salesman of Earl Nightingale's motivational materials, said after hearing a speech I delivered to a group of political campaign workers, "Jim, you have more potential than any young man I have ever known." That statement changed my life. His faith in me exceeded my faith in myself, and I started to explore more of my potential. Thank you, Harold. You made a difference.

Joe Willard, leader of Massachusetts Mutual's Heartland Agency based in Tulsa, Oklahoma, was my first major client and is one of my dearest friends still today. Joe convinced me to stop delivering just generic motivational talks and encouraged me to help people more fully find the potential within them and put it to use.

Tony Alessandra is one of the world's leading speakers and business authors. He is also my closest friend. Tony and I have spent decades helping each other grow. I would not be the person I am today without his influence. His example inspires me daily, and my friendship with him and his wife, Sue, enriches my life.

Earl Nightingale had a profound effect on my thinking. On

x   *Acknowledgments*

tape and in books, his influence on me was immeasurable. Because he chose to develop his nature and become the thought
leader he was, I and millions of others are more than we would
have been.

Paula Cathcart and Jim Cathcart Junior have endured hundreds of hours of listening to me read aloud my latest writings.
Once I pen something, I can't wait to read it to someone and get
reactions. Thanks for being so tolerant of my thought eruptions
and intrusions.

Christine Booth is what I used to call "a brain," she is also
quite beautiful. For four years I worked with Christine to explore the various aspects of being human. Her philosophical and
scientific inquiries led me to some of the foundational conclu-
sions upon which *The Acorn Principle* is built.

Joyce Wycoff, writer and founder of the Innovation Network, spent a full year collaborating with me to write *Third
Thoughts*, a manuscript that preceded this one. Her questions and
translations of my material helped enormously in my ability to
communicate these ideas well.

Rita Derbas is a great thinker. She has worked with some of
the giants of the self-development industry. She spent many
hours reviewing and revising the audio script that foreshadowed
this book. Her keen insight and depth of spirit made a treasured
contribution. Barry Mann, whom I met when he taught acting
at the Old Globe Theater in San Diego, also made gifted edito-
rial contributions to the audio script.

From 1988 to 1991 I owned a part of The Carefree Institute
in Arizona with entrepreneur and researcher Robert Horton.
During that time we collaborated to convert a model he was developing called Profiling into a more marketable form for business related applications. My wife, Paula, renamed the profile the
InnerView™. The differences between the InnerView™ and
the models in the Acorn Profile are many. Some are obvious,
some subtle. For further information on their work, please contact Carefree directly.

Important to the concepts herein are the support and encouragement of the following individuals as well: Jennifer Enderlin at St. Martin's Press; Karen Risch, Wally Bock, my colleagues in Speakers Roundtable; Carolyn Brown, Bonnie Whitman (my marketing director), Gary Goranson, Don Varnadore, and my former coworkers at the U.S. Junior Chamber of Commerce; and, of course, my literary agent, Wendy Keller, of Forthwrite Literary Agency. After my many false starts on this work before I met her, Wendy made this book a reality. She not only opened doors for me, she also kept my faith in this project alive. Thanks, Wendy.

Sometimes the universe blesses you with a very special friend. Such is the case in Dr. Blaine Lee. He generously and meticulously edited this book and, in so doing, raised it to a much higher level of quality and value. Blaine, you strengthen my belief in my own potential. I value your friendship and admire your character.

Foreword

The room was filled. There were probably a thousand people there, and they were all excited. I listened from backstage as the young speaker before me took the microphone. He was only thirty-one years old, yet he spoke as if he were a senior business leader. His confidence in his message surprised and impressed me.

And he was fun! The audience was laughing, taking notes, and responding openly to his questions. Though I was older, more experienced, and more educated than he, I learned something that day from this young man.

That was in the late seventies. Today that young speaker is indeed a senior business leader. Jim Cathcart has authored a dozen books that have been translated into numerous languages. He has owned and built half a dozen businesses, including, for three years, a psychological research firm. Many of the nation's top business speakers regularly turn to him for advice. As president of the National Speakers Association he helped shape the profession both he and I enjoy.

In the following pages you will come to know Jim as I do. You will be captivated by his words and stories. You will see just why I and thousands of others around the world love to learn from this man.

This book is Jim Cathcart's magnum opus. It is the product of his twenty-plus years of research in human performance. It leads you through the process of self-exploration in a way that will excite and please you. You will learn about aspects of yourself that never before caught your attention, and you'll see many new possibilities.

As Jim says, "Intellect is the ability to make distinctions. So to know more, notice more." As a result of reading this book, you will notice more about yourself than 99 percent of people do. In doing so you will also notice more ways to get what you want and ways to connect with others as never before.

Jim adds, "We have three roles here on earth: to learn, to love, and to live. When we stop learning, we start to stagnate and die. When we stop loving, we lose our sense of purpose and become self-centered. When we limit our living, we deny the world the benefits of our talents."

Jim Cathcart will show you how to increase your learning in ways that never feel like work. He will show you how to understand and appreciate others and to connect with them even better. Most of all, he will show you how to live . . . really live! He says, "Our job is to live as fully and abundantly as possible. This means in every aspect of life: mind, body, spirit, emotions, family, friends, career, and finances."

Jim lives what he teaches. He has grown from an undereducated government clerk to a national expert on human development and a world-class speaker and trainer. From his beginnings in Little Rock, Arkansas, and Tulsa, Oklahoma, he has moved to the beautiful California community of La Jolla. He lives by the ocean with his wife of twenty-eight years, rides his motorcycles, writes books, serves on corporate boards, helps others build their businesses, delivers speeches and seminars worldwide, and inspires people like me. His life is an excellent example of how to live abundantly. This book is your key to doing the same.

Read and savor every page. Make Jim Cathcart your friend, too.

Denis E. Waitley, Ph.D.
Rancho Santa Fe, California

Preface

In one growing season an oak will produce thousands of acorns. Some will become food for squirrels. Some will decay and replenish the soil. Still others will eventually become oaks, each of which in turn will produce thousands more acorns. All of them will serve the environment in their own way. What determines their fate?

Each acorn contains within it the potential to become a mighty oak. Whether it does so depends upon a multitude of variables. Weather, soil, insects, diseases, and the behaviors of those around it all have an impact. But every acorn nonetheless contains oak potential.

In the same way, you also carry the potential to have a mighty influence in the world. The seeds of that potential already live within you and around you. In fact, you already have the thought seeds that can make you rich. You already know some of the people who can help your greatest dreams come true. But unlike the acorn, which is at the mercy of the elements, whether *you* fully develop your potential is mostly in your own hands.

You Already Have What You Need to Succeed

People have the capacity to shape, change, or adapt to their circumstances every day. Your life and mine are the result of what we each have done *day to day* with the seeds and circumstances life has dealt us. Everyone is capable of a life of great significance, each in his or her own unique way.

Within you lives a world of potentialities. Talents, ideas, and skills you may not recognize comprise you already. Your success and fulfillment won't depend on changing your nature; they will come from discovering who you already are. You may not fundamentally change, but your use of what lies within you certainly will.

To live the life of your dreams you do not need to be somebody else. You do not need to be smarter than you are or have a different personality. All you need to do to achieve your greatest goals is use what you've got exceptionally well.

The great achievers of our time are not typically people who are fantastically intelligent, amazingly charming, and cunningly manipulative. Most big successes are people who simply apply their natural talents and abilities in intelligent ways. They are people who care about others, are willing to pay their own way, and who refuse to think in terms of what can't be done. For them there is always a way . . . somewhere, somehow.

The same is true for you. If you sincerely want something, the potential to bring it into reality exists within you and in those with whom you can connect. The more you explore your nature, your relationships, and the patterns in your life, the more you will be able readily to tap that potential. Determine what natural gifts you already possess and what resources you already have access to.

In the following pages you will learn a variety of ways to explore and grow the seeds within you. Experts over the centuries have cleared the path for you. The formulas are proven. The process is natural. Know yourself and grow yourself. *An abundant life awaits you. All you have to do is begin to grow, then let the processes of nature guide you toward your own unique potential.*

Like the tree, you, too, have many benefits to give. Your own advancement toward your personal potential will serve the world in ways neither of us could foresee. The added benefit is that you'll have a very good time doing what you are naturally designed to do!

A more fulfilling and impactful life is possible for you without changing who you are. The mighty oak sleeps within you . . . right now.

Introduction:
How to Use This Book

For thirty years the old stock certificate sat in Elizabeth's drawer along with other ancient family papers. She kept it as one would an antique. Then last year she had it framed and hung it in the den. It made a good conversation piece.

When Peter came over for dinner one evening, it caught his eye. He's a financial consultant and owns a local brokerage firm. As he studied the stock certificate, he inquired, "Why is this framed?" She explained that it was worthless and had been around for ages.

Peter was in shock. "Worthless!?" he exclaimed. "Priceless would be more accurate! Look at this official seal. This is one thousand shares of the original issue of Coca-Cola stock. It's worth a fortune!"

How would you have felt if you were Elizabeth at that moment? Rich, yes, but how else would you have felt?

All those years the stock certificate had merely been an interesting piece of paper. Now it was about to change her life in a dramatic way. Absolutely nothing about the paper had changed, but her use of it was certainly going to.

In this book I describe a path to understanding yourself that can change your life in dramatic ways. *The Acorn Principle* is the culmination of nine years of focused personal research combined with decades of research by others. This path includes information from many fields: psychology, biology, organizational development, leadership, behavioral science, systems theory, adult education, and philosophy.

Over the course of these pages we'll venture through what I

believe you need to explore, as well as how. I'll lead you through a series of models each designed to help you know and grow a part of yourself. Each model will lead to discoveries that can cause you to understand and accept yourself as never before.

Why is it important to discover your nature? Because your nature is your essence. It is what you bring into every situation, every thought, every relationship. It is who you are.

As individuals we can activate our self-awareness by looking at our personal core competencies, the things we are naturally suited for. Your individual nature is the seed of silent promise, the acorn that holds great possibilities. The seeds of your future successes already live within and around you.

THOUGHT   BREAK
- Are you today the kind of person that as a child you thought you would be? How are you different from what you expected?
- How will you be different in the future if you make good choices along the way?

If this book belongs to you, I'd like you to write in it now. That's right. In ink, just write today's date and your name anywhere on this page. *The Acorn Principle* is like that old stock certificate. It makes an interesting shelf decoration or conversation piece, but if you really use it as it was designed to be used, it could make you rich in more ways than one!

Let this be your grower's guide for the seeds within your life. Complete the exercises, even ones you have seen or done before. It's important to follow the processes exactly as I've laid them out because all the parts work together. In combination they form a system, and every part of this system contributes to your growth.

Unlike many books that you complete and then set aside, this one continues to give. Write in it. Date your entries. Go back through some of the exercises once or twice a year. *The Acorn Principle* is your guide to a lifelong process of self-exploration. It will help you discover, use, and enhance the best qualities of the seeds within you.

Then call or write me and let me know what value these ideas have brought to you. I am eager to learn from you.

In the Spirit of Growth,
Jim Cathcart
La Jolla, California

Know Your Nature

*D*esire is possibility seeking expression.

—Ralph Waldo Emerson

1. Never Stop Learning About Yourself

With ten hours of hard hiking ahead of us, we were full of excitement. The mountain loomed above us with a smile, as if saying, "Wait till you see the view I have for you!" At a deep stream we faced a choice. We either had to climb down the embankment and wade across, or try to jump the chasm. Neither was very appealing, but we had to do something.

Most of us chose to climb and wade, but one member of the group, Tony, decided to jump. He got a determined look on his face and leaped! He cleared the chasm with inches to spare but fell to the ground writhing in pain. His knee had given out, the one he'd injured in college.

For Tony, the remaining ten hours were pure misery. His injury took all the joy out of the hike for him, while the rest of us had a wonderful climb.

Have you ever done that? Overestimated your physical ability or endurance and ended up injured? How about psychologically? Have you ever miscalculated your ability to think your way through something or underestimated the impact your feelings would have on you? Most of us have.

Self-awareness—knowing your nature, your abilities, and how you'll react to people and things—may well be the greatest life management skill. The better you know yourself, the better decisions you make. The better decisions you make, the better your life will be.

As compared to people who don't know themselves very well, **people who are self-aware:**
- **are better listeners**
- **are less self-conscious**
- **tend to be less judgmental of others**
- **seldom take on tasks for which they are not suited**
- **do a better job of assessing risks**
- **are more willing to admit their mistakes**
- **recover from disappointments more easily**
- **are less likely to be absent from work**
- **tend to produce better quality work**
- **manage stress more effectively**
- **experience fewer interpersonal problems**

In short, people who are self-aware are more likely to succeed and live an abundant life than those who are not. They are also much easier to work with.

Every day you face choices: people to see or not see, places to go, things to do, ways to deal with whatever life gives you. The more effectively you make those choices, the more appealing your outcomes will be.

Someone once asked the famous humanitarian Dr. Albert Schweitzer what he felt was "wrong with people today." He replied, "Most people simply don't think."

On many levels, of course, all of us think. But what most of us neglect to think about is *how* we think. Self-analysis is what is needed. If we were to recognize the patterns in our own thinking and our own feelings, we would understand so much more about ourselves. We could save ourselves a lot of pain by making better life choices and avoiding or redirecting relationships that were destined for difficulty.

Sigmund Freud said, "The trouble with most people's self-analysis is it stops too soon. They are too easily satisfied." That's what *The Acorn Principle* is designed to address: your ability to understand what makes you who you are. As you continue to read and do the simple exercises in this book, you will learn things about yourself that most people not only don't know, they don't even suspect exist!

You'll learn:

- **why some people attract you and others repel you**
- **how to predict your instinctive reactions to various situations**
- **to understand what circumstances you'll thrive in and why**
- **where your intellectual blind spots are in the ways you typically think**
- **why you like or dislike certain things and how to use that knowledge to motivate yourself**
- **who the most influential people are in your life and how to connect with them or others more effectively**
- **how to control your simple daily actions in such a way that you develop new abilities and continually grow a better life**

Maps, Photos, and Guides

Be patient with me on this one; there is a valuable lesson here.

How familiar are you with Mexico City? If left alone to find your way, how well would you do? Your answer would be influenced by a number of factors: your knowledge of the Spanish (Mexican) language, your natural sense of direction, your ability to notice patterns in the streets and architecture for guidance, even your ability to connect and communicate with other people. All would be factors in your ability to get around.

Let's assume your destination is a business office at 101 Avenida Acorn. Think of how you'd search for that address. One way would be to ask directions. If you understood the language, the person guiding you could direct you with relative ease, assuming he or she knew the way.

Another method would be to use a map. The map would not look like the territory you'd be covering, as it would consist of a series of lines, colors, shapes, and words. Still, it would be a great aid for those who know how to use maps.

Once you reached the neighborhood of your destination, you'd rely on address signs, unless you had a photograph of 101 Avenida Acorn. Then recognition would be instantaneous because it would actually look like the photograph.

Now, how familiar are you with *yourself?* How about your closest associates and friends? If left alone to try to understand them, how well would you do?

The principles and tools that guided you around Mexico City can also be used to guide you around yourself and others. You can learn confidently to navigate individual differences and unique personalities. All it takes is a map, a photo, and a guide. One of these without the others would leave you still confused and vulnerable.

A photo is helpful, but without a map, you could search forever in the wrong areas and not stumble upon it. A guide is a great help, but without a map or photo, you are totally dependent on the person. A map shows you much but in no way resembles the actual landscape it describes.

My point is this: To understand a person, first we need an overview of the person with information about his or her key traits. In other words, "John is a male, six feet two inches tall, thirty-five years old, grew up in Texas, speaks English and Spanish, has been trained in mathematics, and possesses a great sense of humor." That's a lot of useful information but nowhere near what you are about to learn.

What if I could show you how to notice the following and more in each person you meet, as well as in yourself?

- **Natural values: the intrinsic motives behind a person's interests and choices—what he cares about**
- **Personal velocity: the pace and intensity at which someone performs best—her "zone" of optimal performance**

- **Multiple intelligences: the unique and varied ways a person is smart—how he is smart**
- **Thinking style (intellectual bandwidth): whether someone tends to think conceptually, strategically, or operationally most of the time and how much information she could effectively process at once**
- **Behavioral style: the predictable patterns within a person's behavior in both positive and negative situations—how he comes across to others**
- **Background imprint: the influences and effects one's experiences have had on her—whether she is working with a head start or a handicap**

If you knew that much about anyone, you would have a tremendous advantage in dealing with him. You could predict what he'd like or dislike, how he would approach a new task, what he'd do under pressure, how he might interpret the behaviors of others . . . and more.

This is precisely what you'll learn as you continue to read this book. *The Acorn Principle* gives you a map, a photograph, and a guided tour of people . . . including and especially yourself. The "map" is a series of models that help you think about human differences. You'll know how to think about personalities and behaviors in ways that not only make sense but also define the best actions to take with each person.

The "photographs" will be exact descriptions and examples of each trait and behavior along the way.

Your "guided tour" will start within yourself. You will do short exercises throughout this book to explore each aspect of your own personality and the personalities of those with whom you are connected.

By the end you'll have a journal full of self-awareness and understand things about yourself that never made much sense before. You will recognize yourself in these profiles. Psychological researchers have a term called "face validity." It occurs when a person reads his or her own psychological profile and says, "Yes, that is me. This profile accurately describes the person I've known myself to be."

In fact, I'll make you a promise. If you read this entire book and work the exercises and then do *not* recognize yourself within the Acorn Profile you will have created—if you don't agree that this process has immensely helped in your self-understanding— then I will personally refund your money. Even if you bought my book from someone else. Just send the book to my office with your receipt and a note that it didn't work for you, and I'll send you a check for the purchase price.

Now that's a fairly bold offer, so let's examine *why you should even care about increased self-awareness.*

Through more than twenty years of conducting training in the area of human development, I have discovered that very few people give much thought to how they think and act or why they are that way. Sure, they occasionally read their horoscope or get a handwriting analysis or call a psychic. But beyond those oc- casional amusements they don't think much about how they think, why they make choices as they do, how they work best, or whom they connect with most effectively.

But if they did think about these things, they might save themselves a lot of unproductive time and effort. One of my fa- vorite examples is Mike, who grew up in a suburb of New York City where his dad was a journalist.

From his childhood Mike wanted to be a writer. However, when he reached college, his best writing efforts brought him only mediocre grades. His confidence wavered, and he switched his major to premed. A natural interest in science carried him through his premed studies, and he was accepted to medical school. In his first year of medical school he tried to quit, but a counselor talked him into staying. His second year of medical school was worse, and again he tried to quit. He hated his third year, so it was back to his counselor who again prevailed. By his fourth year, it didn't make sense to quit, so he finished his med- ical program and became a doctor. Then he quit.

Somewhere along the way, to take his mind off medical

school, Mike started writing again. Before long, he was supporting himself writing thrillers. By the time he finished four years of medical school, he had rediscovered his true passion and was determined to follow it.

Mike is Michael Crichton, and he might have been a pretty good doctor (though his heart wasn't in it), but he became instead a truly great writer when he chose to follow his passion and use his natural strengths. That choice led him to the career of his dreams and a stunning series of best-sellers including *Andromeda Strain, Sphere, The Terminal Man, Travels, The Great Train Robbery, Jurassic Park, Rising Sun, The Lost World, Airframe,* and *Disclosure,* plus the hit television series *ER.*

THOUGHT BREAK

How would you have felt after graduating medical school if you realized that you didn't really want to become a doctor? What would you have done about it? Would you have become depressed and stopped growing, or, like Michael, would you have reached out in new ways to apply what you knew and who you were?

Those who do take the time to explore and nurture themselves have a tremendous edge in the world. For example, imagine that you are a teacher, and a new student comes to you with a significant sense of self-awareness. Imagine the student saying, **"I'd like to learn from you, so here is what I can tell you about me. I tend to think operationally, so I will need concrete examples of the ideas you teach. I can process a few ideas at a time with great efficiency, but my tendency to get confused grows as more ideas are introduced simultaneously. It helps if I can actually do something with the ideas, to make them physical. That is because my physical intellect is higher than my verbal or mathematical intellect. I learn best by doing. My velocity** is fairly low, so please make the learning fun. When it feels like work I tend to become demotivated and easily distracted. My top values are wealth, empathy, and aesthetics. That means I tend to learn best when I can see how something relates to making money or to helping people. And it is most appealing to me when the information is presented in a visually appealing way. By the way, my behavioral style is socializer. I tend to be very vocal and often make jokes while I am learning. This is not meant to be disrespectful; it is just my way of interacting with people. My background was not very supportive so pardon me if, at times, my self-confidence is low. I will take action, but I may need more encouragement than others. The sources I trust the most are authorities and personal experience, so you might want to help me learn from other sources as well. I hope this information will be helpful to you as you teach me."

Many people would find that description a bit overwhelming. Anyone would . . . that is, anyone who had not learned to do an Acorn Profile. You will learn to use the Acorn Profile to understand others as you explore yourself. With an Acorn Profile you will be able to give that much information about yourself in a way that makes others want to help you be successful. Additionally, you will be able to see and understand that much about other people you meet. In this way, you can use your own self-awareness to help others understand themselves. You'll be able to adapt to them and/or help them adapt to you.

2. The Acorn Principle: The Oak Sleeps Within You

You can still feel the indentation in the bark where Dad carved his initials. It lies directly below the spot where my rope ladder used to descend from our tree house. Boy, the times we had as kids!

Now someone else owns the property, and a new crop of kids gleefully pelt each other with acorns. I wonder how many generations of families, birds, squirrels, bees, caterpillars, and earthworms have lived in harmony with that old tree. I love that oak. I've lounged in its shade, climbed its branches, and raked its leaves hundreds of times.

There is something paternal about a big tree. It offers shelter, warmth, shade, and protection from the rain. It changes and grows. As it does, it prevents soil erosion, provides nutrients for insects and animals, and generates oxygen to renew the atmosphere.

Even if you chop it into lumber it lives on, serving others indefinitely.

Do you have a favorite tree? Think back.

What did it feel like to climb it? How did it look? Can you recall the sound it made when the breezes blew? What did it smell like? Trees are powerful symbols in our society. They connect with something deep within us. We feel a natural kinship with them.

The tree is a useful metaphor for personal growth and abundant living. Just as the tree sleeps within the acorn, your future possibilities live within and around you. This book is about finding and developing the natural potential in yourself and others. It is about knowing yourself so well that your life becomes a perfect reflection of your acorn, the seed within you.

The Acorn Principle is simply this:

People Who Know Themselves Grow Themselves.

(People who don't are miserable.)

So know your nature.

The seeds of your future successes already live within and around you.

So explore your nature.

Your greatest, fastest, and easiest growth will always come from your natural abilities.

So nurture your nature.

Because one single acorn grew into a mighty oak, I, my family, and many others benefited. The world is better in both small and large ways because the acorn grew to maturity. Its growth served us as well as itself.

We are all made of "star stuff." When we look up at the night sky and see thousands of bright points of light, or when we look through a telescope and see the face in the moon or the rings of a planet, we are reminded that we are composed of the exact same elements as those fantastically distant stars and planets.

It's awe inspiring to realize that the same atomic and subatomic particles that compose hydrogen, carbon, oxygen, helium, and other elements can either make up a blazing sun or a human being. It's all basic elements. Even more profound is the fact that you are composed of the exact same elements as the greatest people of all time have been. We all share the same basic building blocks, but how we are formed as individuals is what makes us unique.

So what makes you *you*?

Most of us would say, "I'm me because of my parents. I've got my mother's ankles and my father's feet. I've got my grandfather's temper and my grandmother's smile. My family, my heritage makes me *me*."

Another way to answer that question is to say, "I'm me because I've decided to be this way." For instance, your parents may have wanted you to be a doctor, but you decided to become an artist. You consciously chose what you wanted and acted accordingly.

For centuries a debate has raged in philosophical and scientific circles. *Is a person the result of the genetic structures within her, or the result of her environment and her experiences, the process of living?* Is it our nature to turn out a certain way? Were you born with the nature to be a polite person? An artistic person? An angry person? Or were you nurtured into being that way?

This controversy is known as the nature versus nurture debate. I believe that the whole debate itself is a waste of energy because *we are really the result of both our nature and our nurturing.*

Recent brain research has conclusively illustrated that the human brain, as well as the rest of the body, is born with certain predispositions and potentialities. These predispositions are in the form of our genetics and how each brain and body is wired.

While we each have the same elements, they will be put together differently based on how we interact with the world as we develop and grow. Our predispositions or potentialities become full-blown realities only when our experiences activate them. And we find that some potentialities atrophy and disappear altogether if not nurtured during the appropriate phase of their development. *Time* magazine recently featured an article on how a child's brain grows: *"Deprived of a stimulating environment, a child's brain suffers. Researchers found that children who don't play much or are rarely touched develop brains twenty to thirty percent smaller than normal for their age."*

In studies with laboratory animals, researchers found that not only do young rats reared in toy-strewn cages exhibit more complex behavior than rats confined to sterile, uninteresting boxes, but their brains contain as many as 25 percent more synapses per neuron. Rich experiences, in other words, really do produce rich brains. Just as in the biblical story of the talents, the servants who used their talents best were given more of them while the one who didn't had his talents taken away. Nurturing and enrichment are necessary to develop our talents—as the saying goes, "Use it or lose it."

So we are born with certain potentialities—our nature—then we grow from there. We either nurture our nature or prune it depending on the experiences we have and our reactions to them. Sometimes our choices are consistent with our nature; sometimes they're inconsistent with it.

Your Nature Is Bigger than You Think

Late in 1995 the cover of *Time* magazine introduced the world to Daniel Goleman's concept of emotional intelligence, based on his book of the same name.

As you know, intelligence quotient, or IQ, has long been used as a standard for gauging intelligence, which in turn is used as a predictor of success. But Daniel Goleman says that how you handle your emotions is an even more important predictor of success: "I.Q. may get you hired," he writes, "but E.Q. will get you promoted."

In his book, Goleman lists thirteen components of emotional intelligence. The number-one component is self-awareness, how well you know yourself and why you are that way. I have discovered that most people do not know themselves very well. Much of the focus in this book is on looking at ourselves and how we operate.

To begin with, each of us has an internal impulse to become more of ourselves. Aristotle used the term *entelechy,* which means, roughly, a predisposition toward a certain ultimate form. In each life-form's nature is contained its entelechy. "It is the entelechy of an acorn to become an oak, it is the entelechy of a caterpillar to become a butterfly, and it is the entelechy of a baby to become an adult," says philosopher and psychologist Jean Houston, in the autumn 1994 issue of *Noetic Science Review.*

THE NEW BREED

When you truly understand yourself—your nature along with your uniqueness—you begin to see your purpose in life. You also get a glimpse of your amazing potential and begin to sense the completeness that is possible, the oak within you. What's more, you connect with your nature. No outside authority can make choices for you anymore because you replace it with your own inner authority: Now you make choices because you know who you are and what makes sense for you.

Unfortunately, we've been trained to rely on outside authorities to tell us what's right for us or where our potential lies. Let's consider, for example, a person who goes off to a seminar on human development. The seminar presenter sees this person as an acorn ready to grow and says, "Acorn, I believe you've got potential, and I'm going to help you grow into all that you can be. With the right coaching, and if you really apply yourself, I think you could be a giant redwood! [Not a likely outcome.] I've got all kinds of tools and plans for you. Here's a tape I want you to listen to: *The Power of Redwood Thinking* by Dr. Norman Vincent Tree. Listen to that, and it will change your life! And here's a book with the history of some of the great redwoods of all time; learn from their examples. Start networking with the local redwoods, take one to lunch, get to know what they do, watch their patterns. And I've written an affirmation for you; read this along with me: 'I am a redwood great and tall, my mighty branches shelter all. I'm good enough, I'm smart enough, and doggone it, people like me.' "

Now, what's that acorn going to be when it grows up? An oak, that's right, but a really insecure oak! It just got the message it shouldn't have been an oak; it should have been a redwood. Can an acorn actually become a redwood? No. Try as it might, it just can't. However, it can become a mighty oak and impress everyone who sees it—if it develops its own nature.

So what kind of acorn is in you? Have you been trying to be something you were not designed to be? Or have you begun to tap your inner resources and grow? Get to know yourself more fully by studying various aspects of your personality and your life one at a time and then continue this process for the rest of your life. Build a composite self-description, a profile, to determine what kind of seeds you have inside. Then you can learn to master your fate and be much more effective in living a fulfilling and rewarding life.

This process of self-awareness can lead to self-understanding, self-understanding leads to self-direction, and self-direction leads to self-respect, a sense of being worthwhile, capable, and confident. People who understand and respect themselves make better decisions and get along

better with other people. When you've discovered and developed your nature, not only will the rest of the world value and admire you, you'll respect yourself as well.

So how do we learn more about ourselves? The research has already been done for you; all you need to do is apply it. As you explore these various aspects, you will experience profound discoveries that will help explain parts of yourself that you never fully understood before. You'll find lots of possibilities you had forgotten were there. You'll take a mental journey to rediscover and reclaim yourself, and as a result you'll begin to like yourself a lot more. Your behavior and thoughts will begin to make more sense and, for that matter, so will others.

Ask yourself a few questions now.

1. **Which is more important to you: the pay you get for a task or the satisfaction you feel in doing it?**

2. **What is your preference when taking on a big project: to drop everything else and totally immerse yourself until completion or to work on parts of it as you go on with your regular routine?**

3. **Which is more important to you: the ability to learn and explore or the opportunity to become part of a group?**

4. **What do you enjoy most: visualizing outcomes and possibilities or following a tried-and-true process?**

5. **How important is it for you to know where everything is in your world?**

6. **Overall, would you say that you are more or less capable than most people of coping with life's challenges?**

7. **Do you tend to assume the worst so you'll be prepared for problems or do you assume the best so you can see all the possibilities?**

8. **How do you like others to listen as you speak to them: stay quiet or respond actively?**
9. **Which parts of your life are working best right now: mind, body, spirit, emotions, friends, family, career, or finances? Choose three.**
10. **How many people do you consider to be in your closest circle of relationships? What do they all have in common (besides their relationship with you)?**
11. **If you have to know the truth about something, do you rely on individuals, reference books, personal observation, or analysis to find your answers?**

This simple questionnaire provides an enormous window into your nature. Your answers to these questions tell you something about your values, intellectual bandwidth, personal velocity, natural smarts, background imprint, behavioral style, key relationships, life priorities, and preferred sources of information as follows:

#1   measures the wealth value versus the commitment value.
#2   assesses your personal velocity.
#3   pits the knowledge value against the empathy value.
#4   indicates differences in intellectual bandwidth, conceptual versus operational.
#5   checks your behavioral style for steadiness and compliance.
#6   shows self-confidence, which is affected by background imprint.
#7   assesses natural optimism and point of view.
#8   checks your behavioral style as it relates to interaction with others.
#9   highlights where you've been putting the emphasis in your life lately.
#10   focuses on your inner circle.
#11   tests your feelings about the most reliable sources of information.

These are just teaser questions to give you a flavor of the kinds of self-awareness still to come. Don't dwell on your answers to these. This is just an on-the-spot interview. Let it stimulate your curiosity but don't fret over the responses you gave. A more accurate assessment will be made in each chapter of Sections Two and Three.

Let me say right up front that this is not about achieving perfection. At your core you are already perfect in many ways. It is about being yourself—but in the best possible fashion. This is about connecting with your true nature and integrating all its facets—your values, feelings, background, family, friends, and possibilities so that your life really works for you. That's the goal.

Also, let me note what's different about this program from others you may have seen.

Many times when we turn to personal development materials, we want to learn how to apply some new technique or magic formula from some guru, wise person, or outside authority. "Just give me the three steps and I'll be transformed!" Well, that's not what this program is about. This information is based on *your* nature, not mine. You see, you are fine the way you are . . . and you can be even better—by being more *you*! The answers are inside you, not outside you.

The second way this program is different is that this is not information based on one person's opinion. This is not Jim Cathcart's Path to Enlightenment! While I've done twenty years of overall research on this topic, in this text I refer to the works of leading experts in the fields of biology, behavioral science, philosophy, psychology, systems theory, and leadership. You will benefit from not merely one teacher showing you the answers but from many so that you can find your own answers.

Another way this material is different is that it is a source of not just one but multiple methods to explore the many facets of your nature. There are many separate parts of you and me, but all of them are interconnected in subtle ways. **My goal is to help you integrate all these different models into one cohesive**

overview of your unique nature. In future works I will bring you even more ways of exploring yourself. The process is ongoing, and new models are developed all the time to assist in your quest for self-understanding.

Last, this material is different because it looks at your nature from multiple mental, emotional, relational, and physical levels. We look at thinking styles and values, feelings and relationships, and actions and behaviors that you demonstrate in your own style.

All of this combines to offer you an interesting adventure into the nature of your nature—and it is your nature that will determine your life.

My aim is to help you become more of the person you are designed to be, naturally. For most of us that process must begin with a shift in how we think—what the early Christians called *metanoia,* a fundamental shift of mind. The primary difference between happy and productive people and the people who are not is found not just in what they do but also in how they think.

Success in life is not about achieving, it's about *becoming,* becoming the person you were created to be in all the ways you live. When you do that, the achieving is the natural by-product. It is your entelechy to live a productive, abundant, and satisfying life.

3. How Fully Are You Living Now?

One simple question: How fully are you living? How much real, quality living do you do? Do you live life to its fullest?

If you're like most people, there's a lot more living available to you than you're using. Think of all the ways we express our life: relationships, sports, entertainment, creating things, helping others, solving problems, learning, exploring, hiking, loving, boating, looking at the stars, eating good food, celebrating, people watching, reading, drawing, music, watching sunsets, listening to nature, sharing experiences, family, friends, prayer, play, writing, investing, building, and much, much more.

How much living are you doing?

Deep within you lie a multitude of possibilities, your potential. All around you live a multitude of possibilities, your opportunity. Out of all these things you could do, how many are you pursuing? You deserve to be living fully and abundantly.

Think about it. There are people to meet, beaches to walk, stories to tell, songs to hear, wounds to heal, things to say, hearts to touch, minds to fill, solutions to invent, systems to learn, books to explore, letters to read, hugs to give, and ideas to have. The world needs you—really! People are hurting, things are malfunctioning, mistakes are being made, important things are not yet known by others. And there's room for everything to be done even *better*. You were born with many options for being a part of this world, and if you don't explore and express your potential, the rest of us lose the contributions you would have made.

I believe that the purpose of life is to live fully. To achieve this, we must live life skillfully so we can live it more completely and deeply. Otherwise why would we have been given all these possibilities? Your nature is a unique seed that lies dormant until you nurture it.

I recall a story in a scientific magazine years ago that told of the discovery of an ancient urn at an archaeological dig somewhere in Egypt. In the urn were several seeds still intact after centuries of storage. The people studying this find planted some of the seeds as an experiment. To their shock and amazement, the seeds grew! Centuries old and neglected, but with the proper environment they still came to life. It is never too late to grow.

It Worked for Me

In 1975, I weighed two hundred pounds. That's a lot for five feet ten inches of height. For two years I had been active in my community, served on the board of the local Junior Chamber of Commerce, and chaired several projects. My work had been recognized, and I was hired as program manager at the national headquarters of the Jaycees in charge of leadership training, or "individual development," as they called it. All in all I was doing pretty well. My marriage was happy, my career was advancing, and the future looked bright.

One of my assignments took me to Chicago where, along with others, I attended a seminar on personal growth. During the seminar we completed an exercise that had us evaluate each major aspect of our life in relation to the other aspects.

They asked us to rate ourselves on a one-to-ten scale of how effectively we were living in each part of our life: mind, body, spirit, emotions, friends, family, career, finances. What a wake-up call that was! When I realized how lopsided my growth had been (lots of career growth, very little in other areas), I decided to make some changes. And make them I did.

One by one I started exercising, then eating better, getting better organized at work, spending quality time with my wife and son, and joining a self-improvement study group. I persisted through weeks of temptations to quit, just doing a little every day. Within six months I had gotten into top physical shape for the first time ever. I dropped fifty-two excess pounds of fat, enhanced my relationships with my wife and son, organized and managed my finances better, and started making time for spiritual growth, social friendships, and mental development. I even became more creative. Everyone I knew asked, "What has happened to you?" They were amazed (and pleased) at the changes.

Lest you get the wrong idea, this process of transformation was not easy. Simple, but not easy. Over the months of retraining myself and establishing new habits, I experienced many moments of self-doubt, times when I felt unmotivated, and I suffered the pessimism of friends and family on occasion. But the realization of how and where my life was out of balance was just the stimulus I needed to start and sustain a program of daily self-improvement. As I worked to explore and enhance one aspect of my life at a time, day by day my whole life got better. I discovered that when I kept my goals visible to me daily, I found the motivation within me to persist toward them.

Since those days I've significantly refined my process for self-improvement. With more than twenty years of practical experience and lots of formal research, my system is significantly more effective than what I initially used to transform my own life.

What follows in this chapter is a simple yet powerful model you can use to advance any aspect of your life. Step one is a quick self-assessment. Step two is goal setting. Step three, which I will cover in a later chapter, is an action plan I call the "thought diet." Sounds like every self-improvement program you've ever heard of, right?

Yet it really works! I and scores of people I know have used this format to effect profound changes in our lives. No matter how many self-help books you've read or seminars you've attended, if you'd really like to make some changes, you owe it to

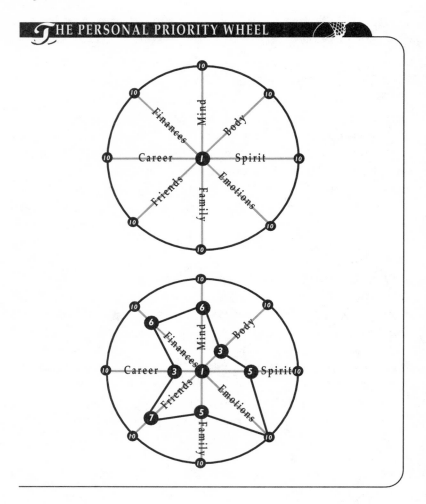

yourself to give this one a try. It could be the beginning of a process that authentically transforms your life.

This exercise is as profound as it is simple. Each spoke of the priority wheel represents a major area of your life. The spoke is also a rating scale for you to measure how fully you've been living in that part of your life lately. The hub of the spoke is zero, and the perimeter is ten. Ten represents living as fully as you could, and zero represents hardly living at all in that category of life.

> Review the following list of ways you live or could live in each category. Then choose a number between one and ten to represent how fully that overall part of you has been living lately. Mark your number on the spoke for each rating scale. Take some time to do this exercise now.

Mind

Your mind is capable of learning, memory, problem solving, creativity, music, poetry, art, writing, brainstorming, and much more. How fully have you been using all the parts of your mind lately? How active have you been keeping your mind lately? How have you challenged it? Choose a number from one to ten.

Body

Your body has myriad functions. Consider these aspects: breathing, blood flow, sensory perception, muscular strength and coordination, balance, overall flexibility and agility, aerobic fitness, nutrition, sex, and healing. Also important to your health are avoidance of poisons such as drugs, nicotine, and alcohol, the use of your body in recreation and sports, relaxation, and repair of the parts of your body that aren't functioning as they should. In relation to your body, how fully have you been living? Do you purposefully take care of your body? Choose a number.

Spirit

Your spirit or soul is the essence of who you are. It's the entity that dwells in your body and uses your mind, the inner you. The spirit awakens and lives through joy and love, inspiration and dreams, vision and commitments. It's nurtured by noble thoughts and inspiring words; it thrives on helping others and on creating things of beauty, works of art. It communicates through prayer and meditation; it honors life. How fully has your spirit been living? Choose a number.

Emotions

There's a multitude of emotions in everyone, including happiness, fear, sadness, joy, compassion, anger, pride, exhilaration, laughter, peace, curiosity, and satisfaction. Are you feeling all these emotions? Or do you suppress many of them? If you're experiencing only a few of these emotions or limiting yourself in how you express your emotions, I think you're missing a lot. We're designed to experience the full range of emotions, not just a controlled few. How fully alive have you been emotionally? Choose a number.

Family

Family describes the people closest to us in life. It can include those who are related to us and those with whom we choose to have a close relationship. In this context I'm referring to the people you love most. Think of the quantity of contact you've had with them, then think of the quality of those contacts. How fully are you living as it relates to your family? Choose a number.

Friends

Your personal community is made up of your friends. Ralph Waldo Emerson said, "A friend is one with whom I may be sincere, before him I can think aloud." We have all levels of friends in life, best friends, neighbors, coworkers, sports buddies, club members, social friends, playmates, and casual acquaintances. Each has his or her place in a balanced, full life. How fully are you living life as it relates to all your friends? Choose a number.

Career

Your career is often called your livelihood. It's often the source of your primary contributions to the world and the source of most of your income, either monetary or otherwise. Is your livelihood lively? As it relates to your knowledge, skills, credentials, achievements, notable contributions, and overall effort, how fully have you been living lately? Do you work to your potential? Do you work with purpose? Choose a number.

Finances

Tangible wealth is usually important only to the degree that you don't have it. Whether or not you are interested in money, it is essential to your survival. And money is not the only source of tangible wealth. Our property and our material possessions also make up our tangible wealth.

Do you know where your wealth comes from, all of it, and where it all goes to in your life? Have you been learning more and more about the use and management of your money? Do you ignore money or stay acutely aware of it? Choose a number to represent how fully alive you've been lately on this scale. Focus not on how much money you have but how fully you have been living in relation to the flow of money in your life.

Well, how did you do? Note the numbers you've chosen.

Once you are satisfied that you told yourself the truth in this exercise, think about what you can learn from this. One thing this exercise cannot tell you is whether you are a "success" or a "failure." Nor can it tell you where you are strong or weak. The ratings cannot tell you anything except what you asked of them. What you asked them was, How fully have I been living lately in this part of my life?

What the ratings do show you is where you have been putting the emphasis in your life.

Add the individual ratings all together and then divide them by eight, since we assessed eight aspects of life. The resulting number will give you an average of how fully you've been living lately overall. Write in that number here along with today's date.

> Number:_____   Today's date: _____

Note what the individual numbers were on each scale. The distance between each of those numbers and the number ten represents the amount of living you could do in that area. If you got anything less than tens all around, then there's plenty of room to grow.

Next, notice which numbers were highest. That's where you've been putting the emphasis lately. That's probably where you are most comfortable.

Now note which numbers were lowest. That might represent areas you avoid or tend to put toward the bottom of your to-do list. Those low numbers represent your most important homework.

Looking over the numbers, you might not see the balanced picture you'd like. In fact, most people do not come up with a balanced circle very often. More often we put our energy into one of the four external areas, like family, friends, work, or finances. We work toward making sure our family is safe, or our job is safe, or our wealth is safe, and then we think we are living fully. Or we spend lots of quality time with our friends and assume that we have a full life. That is not a safe assumption.

You might be just the opposite. The four internal areas are mind, body, spirit, and emotions. Some people put all their energy into making sure they have the body they want. Or they feed only their mind, or nurture their spirit. Others explore and express a multitude of emotions. All of these are important, but advancement in one will not necessarily produce advancement in another. I know a woman who regularly worked out three times a day! She had a great physique but nobody wanted to spend time with her because that's all that she had improved. Her mental, social, and career potentials were seriously underdeveloped.

Grow Each One

If you don't like your ratings, you can change them. Start now to do more of what you are capable of in each area. To live fully, all eight need to be nurtured and in balance. How can you achieve this state?

Take a look at the many ways you use your mind and select one or two for emphasis and development. Then create a simple starting action to get you headed down the path to growth. For example, if you want to be more creative, use brainstorming or a computer game as a daily exercise for a week, then expand from there. To develop your learning, select some learning material and commit five minutes a day to its study. You will usually spend more than the five minutes with it, but even five minutes is probably more than you are doing with that topic now. So get started. In doing so, you'll develop and use more of your mental abilities.

In regard to your body, the main thing is to be active. Like the mind, it's a use it or lose it proposition. No matter what your age, be active physically. Move your body more than you're used to. Even if you do sitting-in-your-chair exercises, move! Movement brings more oxygen to the brain, so you'll even think better.

Feed your body better than you're used to feeding it. Stretch your body and try to do some things that you haven't done in the past; live up to a higher standard when it comes to physical ability. Look to the guidance of organizations like the American Council on Exercise and find out what you can do reasonably for your age and your fitness level to become more and more healthy as time goes on. To have more health, give more activity.

For your spirit, to have more inner peace and joy, give more acknowledgment to yourself for the unique person you are and start to praise others more often. Show more gratitude for what you've received. Give more time to studying what you believe, studying the scriptures or the foundations of the philosophy that you believe in, and give more of yourself to other people, self-lessly.

When it comes to your emotions, if you want more fun, more fullness, more joy, or more peace in your life, then express more of those emotions. A lot of times we isolate ourselves from the rest of the world, and we explore or express only a fraction of the emotions within us. That may be a very comfortable, safe thing to do, but it's not a very rewarding or fulfilling thing to do. And it certainly inhibits your growth as an individual. So look for ways to experience and express more of your emotions and expand your range of experiences.

To have more in the area of family, give more closeness and love. Listen to the members of your family more. Show them more attention; find some little ways to let them know that you care about them. Make some time for them each day. It's amazing how little time we spend with the people we care most about.

In the area of friends, the old line is to have a friend, be a friend. Be a person who's fun to be with. Lighten up and take an interest in what other people are doing. Don't be self-absorbed. Look for ways to support what other people do and to connect with them more. My son said, "If you want to have more mail, send more letters."

From a career perspective, if you want more pay, then first give your employer or customer a raise—do more than you're required to do. If you want more praise from other people, give more compliments to others. Look for ways to add a little bit extra to every customer interaction or to every task or responsibility that you perform. Acknowledge other people for the good job they do. Let your supervisors know what you like about what they do and how they could be even more effective in managing you. If you want more responsibility, take on more responsibility and behave more responsibly in what you do right now.

When it comes to your finances, they say you've got to spend money to make money. Well, that's true only in a limited way. Basically, what you have to do is just take what money and resources you already have and allocate them more wisely or invest your energies in a more financially rewarding way. Think more often about money. Think more responsibly and systematically about money and you'll find ways either to save or earn more. In either case you'll have more money as a result of it.

What will happen as you *give* more energy to each of these eight areas of your life is you will have more life in each of those eight areas. It's your nature to live all aspects of your life fully, skillfully, and with more enjoyment. Nurture that special nature.

Your Highest and Best

In real estate, there's a term called *highest and best use*. This is the optimal purpose to which a property can be developed. For one site, that may be a school, for another a home, and for still another a recreation area or a building. I believe that each *person* is also genetically designed for a highest and best use. Finding your highest and best is a matter of connecting with your nature and growing it, noticing more and more about your needs, your habits, your thoughts, your abilities, and your nature. You were put here for a purpose, and your greatest joy will come from pursuing and fulfilling that purpose. The only limits to what you can be or do are the limits of your nature and the limits of the resources you choose to tap into. What you don't find in one area you can tap into in another. **Magnify your nature by managing your nurture.**

I believe that you deserve to live abundantly. I need what you can do just as you need what I and others can do. It's there for you. Now all you have to do is be yourself, the best self that you can be.

Look at any form of life and you'll find that what it's seeking to do throughout its life is to live more fully, to grow and to thrive. The same is true for me and you. Our genetic purpose is to be fully alive, to tap our potential, explore our possibilities, and ultimately give life to the next generation.

The good news in this is that we're happiest when we're most fully alive.

So if the purpose of life is living, really living, living skillfully, living meaningfully, how do you do it? I suggest that you start with a thorough self-assessment.

Explore Your Nature: A Self-Guided Tour of You

My thirtieth high school reunion was different from the earlier ones. My former classmates were grown up now. Many of them had grandchildren. There wasn't so much strutting and bragging going on. We were more honest with one another.

We had come to accept ourselves much more than before. If we weren't yet living our dreams, we seemed to be matter-of-fact about that and had made our peace with the unfulfilled expectations.

That doesn't mean we weren't still ambitious. Lots of big plans were being made and lives were continuing to unfold. But now the goals related more to what people truly wanted rather than to a vain effort to prove themselves or simply to be "number one."

In a lively conversation with four others, I described my work as a speaker and author. Someone observed, "You always were a natural storyteller." I was? I thought. Why didn't someone tell me that earlier, when it could have made a difference in my career? Instead I had to discover that fact on my own through an elongated process of trial and error spanning many years.

We are all that way to some extent. **What is obvious to others is obscured from our own vision.** That is why the next few chapters of this book will matter so much to you. Each chapter will reveal to you an element of yourself that comprises the oak still within you.

You will explore how you think best, what you care about most, the intensity at which you live most fully, and how you come across to others. Then you'll learn how to assemble this diverse knowledge into a comprehensive self-portrait called the Acorn Profile. This profile will guide you toward better relationships, more effective self-motivation, and higher self-esteem for the rest of your life.

The more you know yourself, the more you accept yourself. The more you accept yourself, the more you accept others. Self-acceptance is the key to personal maturity. Acceptance of others is the key to social maturity. Maturity is no longer what it used to be. In *The Acorn Principle,* maturity means fulfillment of the potential within you, the person you are naturally designed to become.

4. The Living Systems in and Around You

How do I get to know you? If I discover your values do I know you? How about your behavioral style, does that tell me who you are? If I know your background do I understand you? Would it help if I knew your intellect? Would I understand you then? How about if I studied the people you associate with most, do they hold the clue to defining you? How do I get to know *you?*

There is much more to you than any one aspect of your life. You are a network of living systems: nervous, skeletal, digestive, circulatory, skin–nails–hair, lymphatic, musculature, limbic, etc. Each follows a predictable pattern of development and evolves along a natural path. Nails, teeth, hair, skin all seem to renew themselves in the same predictable pattern. If you have a mole on your skin, even though your skin is replacing its cells all the time, it renews itself with the mole still in place. Your fingerprints at birth remain the same throughout your life. Even the hair on your arms seems somehow programmed to grow only to a certain length. Despite exceptions, all these things happen regularly, controlled by some genetic code locked into our cells.

But if I want to know the real you, how do I read the genetic code, what do I focus on? Your looks, your voice patterns, your body posture, your mannerisms, what? Where exactly is what is known as *you?*

Some say you're in your brain, some say your heart, some say your mind, some say your spirit. Which is accurate? What's the difference among mind, brain, heart, and spirit? Which contains your personality? Tough to answer, eh?

It gets worse. If we answer, "It is in your personality," how do we define or isolate personality? Perhaps by behavioral style? But what about your system of values, your thinking style, your learning style, your various intelligences, your personal velocity, your background's imprints on you, or your preferred information intake mode (often called neurolinguistic programming)?

Could we look outside of you for the answers? Perhaps the answers are in your circle of relationships or in the way you were raised. Could it be the generation in which you grew up? Maybe in astrology, numerology, culture, religion, biorhythms, or some form of mystic study that holds the clue? Still we are left seeking the answer to, "Where are you?"

Generally you tend to be wherever your body is. But your consciousness transcends your physical limits. Again and again we encounter documented accounts of a person "knowing" something that is beyond his or her physical capacity to sense it. Years ago I called my mother, who is in Arkansas, from my home in California. I told her I had been in bed with pneumonia for five days. She exclaimed, "It was you! I've had a strong feeling for days that Jimmy [my son, her grandson] was in trouble. But it was you!"

Somehow she knew her child was in danger. Think of people you've known who've also experienced ESP or extrasensory perception. It is not magic or mysticism but simply the experience of perceiving something beyond our five senses. All of us have had some experiences of intuition, or gut feelings we couldn't explain logically. The trouble is that most of us don't have the right words or understanding to discuss and examine those experiences intelligently.

Our Western culture has, for decades, regarded people as machines. We tend to separate mind, body, and spirit as we would separate a hermit crab from the shell it chose to occupy. It's as if the dominant belief is: Your body is the real you, and your mind is what your body uses to direct itself. This assumes that your mind is merely a function of your body.

Our intentions are part of our behaviors. Our thoughts manifest as our actions but not always in obvious ways. Thomas Merton once said, **"The thought manifests as the word. The word manifests as the deed. Deeds form into habits. And habits harden into character. So watch your thoughts with care."**

How do we truly understand each other when there are so many levels on which we operate? Every one of us is an integrated network of living systems, each changing from day to day but always following a natural path of evolution. These living systems that comprise us are so many and so complex that it is virtually impossible to completely understand them. The truth is, there is no fixed location that can be defined as "you." You are a work in progress, a dynamic living system. And you function within a series of other living systems. So when you study "you," you are not studying a painting or photograph that never changes, you are studying a moving picture from every conceivable camera angle. The best any of us can do is sustain a *lifelong* process of self-exploration. Only by continually noticing more and more about ourselves will we come to understand who we truly are. The following chapters will guide you in the discovery of a variety of the elements that comprise you. Each chapter will focus on only one aspect of you, but all of them must be taken together in order to really know yourself.

All Parts of a System Are Vital Parts

My mother-in-law once had open-heart surgery. As I sat in her hospital room with the family during a visit by her doctor, a question hit me: What will contribute the most to her recovery? The medical system that serves her, the natural systems within her body, the belief systems by which she operates, or the support system of those of us who love her?

The answer, of course, is that all of these are necessary. Without any of them doing its job well, she couldn't fully recover. Likewise, all the fields of philosophy, science, medicine, biology, psychology, and systems design overlap in ways that a discovery in one area can lead us to a deeper understanding of the other areas. It's time to expand our thinking, to see ourselves not as a separate entity but as a part of a system within other systems. In doing so, we open up unlimited possibilities.

When we learn to use the systems by cooperating with them and orchestrating what's within them, we can achieve virtually all we desire.

One useful way to think about systems is to think about a rain forest versus an orchard. Each is a system, but the rain forest is a much richer and more complex system, perpetuating itself naturally. The orchard, on the other hand, has to be maintained artificially by a farmer or gardener. It can be threatened by one disease that could wipe out the entire crop, whereas the rain forest may have a thousand insects or diseases invade it and still persist because it has so many aspects, each performing its own function, in an overall, well-coordinated ecosystem.

What is true of the rain forest is true of our society, our businesses, our families, and ourselves. There are many, many parts of who we are, and the more of those parts we discover, the more effectively we can guide our living to be abundant in all the areas of our life.

Everything I do and everything I don't do affects other people, and likewise I'm affected by them. If I contribute my part, everything goes fine. If I do not contribute my part, I increase the burden on other people. For example, if I hear an alarm go off and take no action, someone else has to act or the emergency goes unheeded. In society, if you're not helping to pull the wagon, then you're riding in it and making the load heavier for those who are pulling it. In a system, all parts are vital parts.

THOUGHT BREAK

How many systems are you a part of? How many systems are a part of you? List as many as you can. Discuss your list with others.

5. The Seven Natural Values: Discovering What You Care About (Why You Want What You Want)

Years ago I lived in Tulsa, Oklahoma. I remember talking one day with a friend about the topic of motivation. He told me that if we could ever figure out how really to motivate people, we could make a fortune. But those who have taken any leadership training at all know that people do things for their own reasons, not for yours. And that's the real definition of *motivation*: It means to stimulate a *motive*. So if we want to motivate somebody, what we've got to do is not come to him with motivation but rather look inside him for *his* motives.

Primary motives develop very early in life, as do other individual characteristics. Have you ever noticed the differences in infants even when they come from the same parents? A lot of times I will ask my audiences to comment on how different their babies were one from the other, and they'll cite differences of all types. I'll ask, "At what point in the second child's life did you notice that this child was really different from the first one?" Some people say the first year, others say six months, still others say at birth. One person even said, "I think I could tell about halfway through the pregnancy."

There are differences in how active the children are, how they take their food, how they respond to touch, how they interact with others, how they relate to their toys and their environment, and many other things. These differences become even more pronounced as they mature. Therein lies the key to people's motivation.

There are two kinds of motivation, extrinsic and intrinsic. Extrinsic motivation occurs when we try from the outside to provide a motive for some action or behavior. For instance, you might say to your child, "If you pick up the toys in your room, you can stay up thirty minutes later tonight." Or maybe your sales manager decides to give a bonus to the person who brings in the most money in a month. That's extrinsic motivation—the outside trying to get the inside excited.

Intrinsic motivation occurs when we are moved to action because of our internal motivation. For instance, maybe when you were a kid you really wanted a new bike but your parents said they wouldn't pay for it. You decided that somehow you would earn the money to buy the bike. So you got a paper route, sold cookies door to door, baby-sat, or started a lawn-mowing business, anything to get that money because you really wanted that bike. You were internally motivated to find a way to get the money.

That's intrinsic motivation—when we make a conscious effort to achieve a goal because we want it, not because someone else sold us on it. *The secret to great leadership is to find out what the intrinsic motivations of your followers are, then gear the extrinsic motivators to appeal to those.* And the key to intrinsic motivation is in a person's value system, because values shape who you are and direct why you do what you do.

Each of us has a unique set of values. *Value* denotes the importance of something relative to other alternatives. Values are what you care about, the qualities you find desirable. Values are not attitudes or behaviors, though they form the basis of our attitudes and behaviors. Every decision we make is based on our own set of values.

For example, some personal values are loyalty, wisdom, love, honesty, justice, and many more. When we make a decision or when we act, we usually do so in accordance with our personal value system. Now, I don't want you to confuse values with virtues. Virtues are standards of excellence, morally the *right, best* actions to take. With values, however, we look at what you care about most, right or wrong, good or bad.

I'd like to focus on a value system model based loosely on the works of Edvard Spranger of the University of Berlin and the more contemporary work of Gordon Allport. I initially developed this system in concert with Robert Horton of the Carefree Institute to build on some of the seminal work Horton did with Dr. Pat Fellows on what they called "the Pars." Since then I've retitled it the Natural Values model.

In this research I have found seven values that are common to everyone. These aren't values we've learned; rather, they're part of who we are. These seven natural values are with you at birth and stay with you throughout your life. These values are in the acorn, part of your very nature. They are as follows:

- **Sensuality**—the relative importance of one's physical experience
- **Empathy**—the relative importance of feeling connected to other people
- **Wealth**—the relative importance of ownership and worth
- **Power**—the relative importance of control and recognition
- **Aesthetics**—the relative importance of beauty, balance, order, and symmetry
- **Commitment**—the relative importance of being committed to something, having a cause or mission, doing the "right" thing
- **Knowledge**—the relative importance of learning and understanding

You and I share all seven of those values, but if we were to rank which ones were most important to each of us, your top values may be different from mine. If my top value is power and yours is knowledge, we will respond to a stimulus in different ways.

For example, say our employer offers us a chance to attend a seminar on value systems. Your main reason for attending might be simply to gain the knowledge because you love to learn—you have a high knowledge value. But if my highest value is power, my main reason might be to find ways to use this new knowledge to advance my position and better lead my team.

We both would benefit from the training, but we would have different primary motives for learning what was taught. If commitment were my main value, I would go to the seminar because it was the right thing to do, or because it was a way to show my commitment to the organization. If empathy were your main value, you'd probably be attending to find new ways to connect with your people and help them more.

If sensuality was your main value, you might want to attend so you could be in a new surrounding with a new meeting room or new environment. With aesthetics as a main value, you might attend because of the beautiful location of the seminar or the architecture of the building. A high wealth value would cause the seminar to be seen as a vehicle for gaining more worth in the marketplace. Is this starting to make sense?

None of the values is better or nobler than the others in and of itself. It's how they're acted upon that determines that. **Our values don't determine *whether* something will appeal to us nearly as much as they determine *how* that thing will appeal to us.**

I might like a certain desk because of how it feels to sit at it, or I may not like the desk because it doesn't feel right—that's sensuality. You may like it because of its looks, or you may not like it because it doesn't look like you think a desk should look—that's aesthetics. Paula may like its prestigious style and brand name—that's power value. Bonnie may like the fact that her best friend has one just like it—empathy. For James it may symbolize the value of his contributions to the company—commitment. For Wendy, the rich mahogany desktop and its value as an antique might appeal to her wealth value. Same desk, totally different reasons for liking it.

On occasion a certain item might attract one person and repulse another. If Janet received a large new executive desk and her colleagues didn't, her high empathy value might cause her to feel unnecessarily separated from the group. The same desk could appeal to Don's high power value. He might love the distinction of standing out from the crowd.

Incidentally, there's no importance to the sequence in which I've listed these values. The reason they're listed this way is because they're easy to remember if you use the acronym SEW PACK: Sensuality, Empathy, Wealth, Power, Aesthetics, Commitment, Knowledge. Think of those little sewing kits that they give you as an amenity in a hotel room. Picture one with seven different colors of thread. The threads hold things together. Each color does the job as well as the other, but their difference is noticeable to the naked eye. This analogy gives you a convenient way of remembering the words.

Seeing and Hearing the Values

People show their values all the time through what they say and don't say, what they do and don't do, what they approach and what they avoid. Here are some indicators to watch for to identify people's top values.

Sensuality. A person with a high sensuality value shows an interest in and affinity for physical experience: taste, touch, smell, fit, comfort, temperature, texture, humidity, sound, volume, light, etc. There's a sensitivity to the physical aspects of an experience that stands out for this person. He or she might choose a certain restaurant for the feel of its dinnerware or its seating comfort as well as for its food.

Empathy. People with a high empathy value need to be around other people they care about. The helping impulse is very strong in these folks. They're drawn to the needs of others and are sensitive to their reactions and experiences. They may buy a product as much for their sense of connection with the salesperson as for their actual need for the product.

Wealth. People with a high wealth value find that the worth of a thing or its fair price value matters a great deal. They may wear an expensive ring even though they don't particularly care for how it looks. The sincerity of one's words is often evaluated by these people through looking at what they do with their money. "Do you put your money where your mouth is?" they ask. People with a high wealth value really care about accumulating things, because that's how they evaluate how things are going. It's not greed to them; it's just putting value on acquiring or owning things of quality. They believe that the profit motive is a perfectly legitimate basis for any business.

Power. People with a high power value find acknowledgment, praise, special privileges, honors, titles, and prestigious things of prime consideration. Position and control matter a lot. These people evaluate information by its source, the title, the position the person holds. They may find the fact that they were seated in the VIP section even more pleasing than the concert. High power value types love to be in charge.

Aesthetics. People with a high aesthetic value would find beautiful sunsets, organized systems, certain color combinations, paintings, landscapes, and architecture of strong appeal. The look or graphic layout of your proposal may carry as much impact as its contents from their point of view. They may feel that the meeting would have been much more productive if it weren't in such a dull looking room. People with a high aesthetic value truly care how things look and feel. They want to make life aesthetically pleasing, whether that means reorganizing things or increasing the beauty of their surroundings.

Commitment. People with a high commitment value have strong convictions. Beliefs and affiliations are at the center of their attention. Working to advance a cause, crusading, and campaigning feel good to them. These people do things because they feel they are the right things to do. They like being part of an organization or a group that they believe in. As a matter of fact, to them, it's critical that they believe in it. They make statements like, "I trust her because she demonstrates her commitment. If she says it, you can take it to the bank." They willingly make sacrifices in other areas to do what they feel is right.

Knowledge. People with a high knowledge value love to learn. Knowledge is valued as an end in itself. Books, seminars, discussions, and problem solving are things they enjoy. They may tend to listen to learning tapes or public radio rather than music stations. They seem to have an endless curiosity, being constantly amazed at how little they know on each subject. They say, "So many books, so little time." Someone with a high knowledge value considers going to a seminar a benefit in and of itself whereas someone with a lower knowledge value might find it to be a burden, an inconvenience.

Behaviors That Grow from Each Value

Certain behaviors are driven by our value system. Here are some characteristics for each value. See which ones you identify with.

High sensuality value. These are people who are acutely aware of their physical experience. Before they get involved with a task they take a few moments to get comfortable, what in the South we used to call "fixing to go to work"—adjusting the chair, adjusting the computer screen, getting their tools in order, and so on. They tend to be touchers, enjoying very much the physical aspects of everything. They go out gourmet dining to enjoy the taste of the food, the texture of the silverware, the smells from the kitchen.

Everything they do is experienced initially through a sensual filter. They are drawn to physical experience, easily distracted by their senses. They could be gourmets, fitness enthusiasts, auto mechanics, bungee jumpers. High sensuality is a noticeable value ranging from passive sunbathing to the excitement of downhill skiing.

High empathy value. Empathy leads a person to be more compassionate and understanding of others. A *New Yorker* cartoon showed a boardroom in which one fellow was hugging another one and saying, "Oh, that was a wonderful report, Bob, a wonderful report!" The caption read, "Vice President in Charge of Sincerity." Well, people with a high empathy value tend to be that type. They often feel it's better to give than receive and are willing to take care of other people's needs before their own.

David Dunn wrote a beautiful little book called *Try Giving Yourself Away.* In it he says, "I know that the little surges of happiness I get out of giving myself away suffuse me with a momentary sense of glowing health. I've come to believe that my hobby of helping, of giving away, with the flush of pleasure it brings, is the finest heart tonic in the world."

High wealth value. People with a high wealth value demonstrate a maximum interest in the security of their money. They direct their efforts toward their job and economic security. They want to know about benefits, bonus plans, stock purchase plans, retirement plans, etc. They'll work at a job they don't enjoy as long as the pay is good, because their primary motive is wealth. As far as they're concerned, the profit motive is a valid basis for work as well as a legitimate organizational purpose. Ask them what's the purpose of your business and they'll say to turn a profit. They prefer tangible goals with financial numbers attached to them. They really dislike monetary waste; a spendthrift makes them very uncomfortable.

High power value. People with a high power value exhibit two elements, control and recognition, as primary appeals. They want to be in charge of whatever they're involved in, love to get things done and meet schedules, eliminate disagreement and questioning. They are intolerant of errors and tend to blame others. They like direct confrontations and enjoy winning arguments. It's not that they're mean-spirited; they just enjoy being in charge and making things happen. They also like to be the center of attention; as a matter of fact, they can seldom get enough of that. I would imagine that Elvis Presley had a very high power value. For that matter, apparently so does the real estate baron Donald Trump. I'm sure you can think of many people in the news who fit the behavior patterns of this value.

Additional characteristics of these people are that they tend to avoid situations where their achievements won't be recognized. They need regular reinforcement, like to display status symbols, and strive for fame or accomplishment.

High aesthetic value. People with a high aesthetic value are drawn toward beauty, harmony, balance, blend, symmetry. They're distracted by disorder or ugliness, they feel a need for closure, they like systems and structure, they like the completion of an act. Everything in its place, a place for everything, works for them. It doesn't particularly have to be neat and tidy, but it does need to fit together nicely. These people are more likely to be artists at what they do, even if that's mathematics or computers. They seem to be deeply moved and renewed by exposure to beauty.

High commitment value. People with a high commitment value really think that doing what you believe in is the essence of being a good person. They live a purposeful life and will sacrifice for their ideals and standards. Doing what's right takes precedence over doing what works best. They tend to be fatalistic, saying, "It was meant to be." These folks have a zealot's enthusiasm for what they do, turning it into a religion on some levels.

High knowledge value. Those with a high knowledge value have an intense drive to discover. They need a way to explain things in the world and want to better their situation through learning more. They are seekers of the truth, wanting to make sense out of things. They continue their quest for knowledge and discovery even when their own safety is threatened. They are the types who make good newspaper reporters because they'll keep probing and asking and exploring, trying to find the information they need.

Back to the *New Yorker* magazine: Another cartoon showed a man sitting beside his son's bed, obviously reading him a bedtime story but handing him some papers in the process. The caption read, "Then Jack traded his cow for five magic beans. Here's a copy of the contract, the accounting summary, the insurance waiver, the shareholders briefing, and the receipt."

What About You?

Now, what about your own top values? I'm sure you've been thinking about them throughout this chapter as I've listed them—it's a natural impulse.

> Here is a quick values check you can do. Answer the following five questions in writing. Quickly write what first comes to your mind. Trust your gut reaction.
> 1. What qualities do you most admire in a friend?
> 2. What traits do you most want in a mate?
> 3. What do you think kids should be taught in schools?
> 4. If you could change the world in some way, what would it be?
> 5. If you won the lottery and money was no longer a limitation to you, what would you do with the money?

Look over your answers, then look back at the seven natural values and look for matches. What you'll find is that the values tend to pop to the surface in your answers. Which values were expressed most strongly? Those questions all had the same basic inquiry—what do you care about?—but they asked it from five different points of view.

Once you've evaluated your answers you'll have a pretty quick sense of what your top few values are.

If you think you've figured out someone else's values and you want to apply some extrinsic, outside motivation in accordance with his or her intrinsic values, here are some incentive or gift ideas to appeal to those values.

Sensuality value. Appeal to her senses. Give her a dining certificate to savor a good meal, or membership in a spa so she can enjoy all the attention. Take her on a sports outing, on a ski trip, sailing. Give her tennis lessons, golf equipment, fitness coaching, custom clothing, or better tools to work with.

Empathy value. Give him ways to demonstrate his high empathy. He might like time off or flextime so he can spend time with friends or give personal advice or participate in a collaboration. Involve him in team activities, include him in a special group of people like himself, give him the chance to help someone he cares about. Hold a social in his honor with his special friends.

Wealth value. Give her money: gold coins, cash, stock certificates, investment advice, membership in an investment group, seminars or books on money, financial management software, a subscription to a financial magazine or a collector's newsletter. Money motivates people with a high wealth value. But be creative in the way you provide it. Money may not be the only way they identify with wealth. They may find wealth in antiques or in money-saving tips.

Power value. The sort of things that would appeal to this person are whatever he perceives as a mark of power. What does your organization use as a sign of power? A bigger office, special parking privileges, a title on the business card? Can you include him in a prestigious group? Give him a chance to run things, more responsibility. Publish a profile of him in the company magazine, engrave his name on the producer-of-the-month plaque, praise him in front of others, give him a trophy or certificate.

Aesthetic value. This person really loves to help make things more beautiful, whether it's redecorating a lobby or redesigning a newsletter. Give her an opportunity to show off her sense of balance and beauty. As a reward, how about a trip to an art exhibit, a new filing system, membership in an art society, a painting or sculpture, an office with a better view, designer services for her office or home, a class in art or architecture, custom designed jewelry, new drapes or wall coverings?

Commitment value. Give him time off to pursue a campaign of some sort that he believes in, give him input on policy making, give him a way to show his commitment to the organization through extra effort, delegate things to him and rely on him more. How much you rely on him, of course, depends on his level of mastery. But give him a chance to be more significant to the organization or the people within it. Build on the fact that he loves to work for a great cause or serve on a campaign of some sort.

Knowledge value. Buy her books. She loves to learn, so give her a chance with a library card, seminar enrollment, access to a mentor, personal training, a coach, learning software, participation in a discussion group, some education she wants to get. It will appeal to her primary value and draw her more strongly in the direction you would like her to go.

You could conceivably spend the exact same amount of money on each of seven different people but provide a different reward for each one of them.

You might say, "I'd like most all of the gifts and privileges listed above, and so would many others I know. What is so special about giving according to values?"

Here is what makes it special: Everyone enjoys good things, but the things that are aligned with our values we not only enjoy, we cherish! **The quickest way to someone's heart is through his or her values.** With an ear to noticing someone's values, new ways to tailor your gifts, motivation, incentives, and rewards will become obvious to you. You'll see not only how to increase the appeal but also add impact to your leadership. **People will be more likely to follow your lead because your lead follows their values.** This applies to parents, managers, salespeople, everyone.

To understand somebody and know how to use this value equation to relate to him or her, all you really need to notice is his or her top few values. If you know the top two or three, you've got enough to understand how you can appeal to him or her with whatever idea you are presenting.

The $10,000 Painting

There was a man who had a very high aesthetic value, and his lowest value was wealth. He was married to a woman who had a very high wealth value, and her lowest value was aesthetics. They were exact opposites on a values level. Both of them were doing very well in sales, with her working in a financial institution and him in a software company. One day he made a sale that was so large that he received a $10,000 on-the-spot cash bonus! You talk about a great day—this guy was thrilled. He took his money and said, "We're in pretty good financial shape. This is mad money; I can do whatever I want with it." He had a high aesthetic value, so he immediately ran down to the neighborhood art gallery and spent the entire $10,000 on one painting.

He had the painting brought to his home and installed it in the living room. (You don't hang a $10,000 painting, you *install* it.) He readjusted the lighting, rearranged all the furniture, and got the room just right, so that no matter where you were, you could see the beauty of the painting. He was standing there basking in the glow of his new acquisition when his wife came home.

She walked in the door and said, "What's that?" He said, "It's a painting. Come here and look." She said, "Did you buy that?" He said, "Yeah, come here and look." She said, "What did it cost?" He said, "Notice these little delicate brush strokes." She said, "Come on, don't avoid me, what did it cost?" He said, "Um, uh . . . ten thousand dollars."

Well, she hit the ceiling. "How could you do that, ten thousand dollars for something on the wall?!" He went into a panic. He didn't know what to do. He was thinking, *How do I get her off the ceiling?* Then he remembered natural values.

So he said, "Honey, can you see the painting from up there?" She looked down from the ceiling and saw the painting. He said, "Notice the artist's name. Yeah, I thought you would recognize her name. That artist's work has been appreciating at thirty percent a year for the last three years, and she was just featured on the cover of *People* magazine." Upon hearing that, his wife slowly drifted back down to the floor, looked at the painting, paused, and said, "Notice how it brings out the colors of the couch."

Did he change her values? No, he merely *understood* her values and showed her how what he cared about—the painting—related to what she cared about—the money. And the minute she saw that the money side of the equation was handled, all of a sudden her lower-value aesthetics could be appreciated.

What we care about most drives our interest and our criteria for decisions. So your highest values cause you to focus on certain aspects of a situation and overlook others until you've handled whatever it is you're concerned about on your top values. Only then can you effectively focus on the other parts of it. The better we understand what's important to others, the more we can attune our own preferences and information to their top values, and we'll be working in alignment with them from the start.

THOUGHT BREAK
- What values from the list of seven did you identify with strongest?
- What top values would you say your parents had?
- What values do you demonstrate in your work environment? Are they the same ones you demonstrate outside work?
- How can you better nurture your values?
- What are your top three values? Bottom three?
- How do your top values differ from your mate's?

6. Finding Your Zone of Optimum Personal Velocity

Remember the fable of the tortoise and the hare? The hare ran very fast but got cocky and slacked off, then lost the race. The tortoise moved slowly but consistently and won the race. The tortoise and the hare is an excellent metaphor for understanding the nature of our individual velocity.

Velocity? Most people don't think about having a personal velocity. Velocity, which is rate of motion or speed, is usually used in the context of a car or a speeding bullet, not in the context of a person.

But I'd like you to think for a moment about your personal velocity. What is your velocity? That's an interesting question, isn't it? *Your velocity is a combination of your energy patterns and your drive.* There's a natural intensity and drive, a pace at which each person is at his or her best, and it differs from one individual to the next.

So what's your natural pace? In order to find out you'll need to understand the concept of human velocity. Velocity is the intensity with which you live. Some people naturally operate at a highly intense pace and others at a less intense pace. Each is probably best suited to his or her own pace. But in our society we have a bias toward achievement and encourage each person to aspire to high velocity. That may or may not be a good idea.

In business we have sales contests that reward the short-term achievers who did the most. Sports and games acknowledge those who give it an all-out effort. Schools and businesses recognize people who produce big results in a short time frame. Is that bad? No, but there should also be some time and energy devoted to those who don't operate at such a frenetic pace. If they contribute to the advancement of the business or society, they should also be acknowledged for doing so.

Let's look at your natural pace, your natural velocity. There are three different levels of velocity.

In my family we have an example of all three levels of velocity—high, moderate, and low. You might have already guessed that my natural velocity is high. I love to work long hours and tackle big assignments. My spare time is also spent advancing my goals. I consider it fun. For me, a typical goal involves world-class achievement, like having an influence on humanity. Very ambitious, I'll admit, but I like huge goals. People used to say to me, "Jim, don't get your hopes up." But I love to get my hopes up! It gives me energy and fills me with life. Sometimes I don't reach my goals, but sometimes I do. And when you're reaching really big goals, that's absolutely fun.

My wife, Paula, has moderate velocity. She's much less intense than I am, thank goodness. When she was in the workplace, for

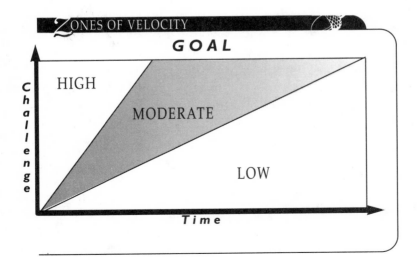

her a normal workday would be eight hours. She'd put in overtime if she needed to, but she wouldn't put it in because she felt compelled to; she'd put it in because it was needed as part of the team's contribution to the effort. Her way of working is to identify a particular time frame for the various things that need to be done and to do it within that time frame. If it doesn't all get done today, there is still tomorrow.

My style is to take on a huge project and just keep on working as long as I can reasonably work and enjoy the work the whole time. I don't exhaust and overwork myself, but I love to have lots to do, a big challenge. Paula, on the other hand, would prefer to set more reasonable goals that she has a pretty good certainty of achieving. Her way of doing it would be to lay out a simple plan and follow the plan pretty much systematically. She's not a detailed planner, but then again she doesn't have to be because she's good at what she does.

In his teens, our son, Jim Junior, showed much lower velocity. His pace was easy and laid-back; he's a mellow kind of a guy. He never was the type who would get really excited about a long-term plan for a big goal. For him, setting the next goal, the next reasonable achievement, seemed to make better sense, and he liked to go with the flow.

Years ago when he was just a young guy, I would look at him and see that he was doing fine yet still feel the need to motivate him. He was playing soccer with a team that was doing really well, and a couple of times they won the local championship. He was making good grades in school, he ran around with a good crowd, and he was liked by virtually everybody. What more could I want? But the one thing that bugged me (remember, I'm a motivational speaker) was that he just never set a really big goal and went after it with commitment!

I thought the boy needed repair. I decided I would fix him. So the first thing I did was start watching him more closely to identify a motive. I figured if I could identify a motive within him, then I could activate that and he would be much more of an achiever.

As I set about watching for a motive, one day he laid one right in my lap. He said, "Hey, Dad, you used to play the guitar in cocktail lounges and night clubs. Would you teach me how to play the guitar?" I said yes and started licking my chops! I grabbed my spare guitar, gave it to him, and handed him a song-book with lots of chords in it. I said, "I want you to start learn-ing these. Do this until your fingers bleed, then rest a day, and we'll do it again the next day. I've set you up with a couple of meetings with a guitar instructor." I then proceeded to lay out a three-year plan.

I overwhelmed the guy. It was as if he had asked me for a sip of water and I'd drenched him with a fire hose. It took him about ten days to lose all interest in the guitar. I had so over-whelmed him that he didn't want to pursue it anymore. I thought, *Well, it was just a weak motive; I'll wait for another one.*

Now and then after that, he would come up with another motive and I'd come up with some sort of three- to five-year plan. Every time he'd show the little flame I would douse it with a huge plan that was way too big for the interest he had ex-pressed, and after a while he just stopped asking. He wouldn't come to me with questions or motives anymore; instead he'd go to his mom.

One time he went to Paula and asked, "Hey, Mom, what's the answer to this?" She said, "Jim, why don't you ask your dad?" He said, "Mom, I don't want to know that much!" Oops. Well, I finally figured out what I was doing wrong. I started listening to him more and giving him his answers in bite-sized pieces rather than great big truckloads. As I did so, he got better at things, immediately. Once I learned about his natural intensity and acknowledged his preferred pace, I was able to align my plan with his natural velocity.

His velocity is not like mine. It didn't make sense for me to take on things the same way he would take on things, or expect him to take on things in the same style I would.

A few years later he was off at college. A friend of his said, "Would you like to learn to play the guitar?" He looked around to see if I was watching (I wasn't), and he said yes! So the friend taught him some guitar techniques, just a few basic ones, and asked, "What's your favorite song?" By providing Jim with an application of his favorite song along with those techniques, he had a *why* behind the *how,* a *reason* to learn the chords and techniques. He started playing his favorite song, practiced until his fingers got sore, the next day got up and practiced again, and after a while built up the calluses so he could keep on playing.

Today he's a qualified guitar technician and amateur songwriter, and has worked occasionally with a band in Los Angeles. When he plays guitar, he can sit down in front of a radio and play along with the music. And when he comes home on holidays he teaches me guitar techniques. The student has become the teacher.

Did Jim's velocity increase? No, it didn't. He just figured how to get what he wanted, accomplishing it at his own pace. As long as he was *playing* the guitar and not *working* it, then he was learning and enjoying. But when it started feeling like work he'd set it aside and do something else.

Why did Jim Junior learn when his friend taught him and not when I taught him? I think it's because I was rushing at my personal velocity to give him all the techniques I had learned, all the knowledge I had, and expected him to learn at that pace. What I forgot totally was his personal motivation, his intrinsic motivation. The friend started with a song that Jim *wanted* to learn, and the friend let him learn at his own pace. That made all the difference for Jim Junior.

How you view work may also be a key to understanding your personal velocity. People of low velocity generally don't enjoy anything that feels like work. They would gladly follow the philosophy that you should make your play your work and your work your play, meaning that they'd love to make a living doing what they love. Wouldn't we all?

People of high velocity, on the other hand, actually enjoy the work, as long as it moves them toward their goals. They some-

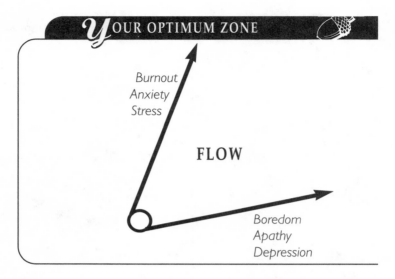

times get bored with play and feel the need to turn play into work. They need that intensity and purposefulness. In contrast, moderate-velocity people like a nice balance of work and play.

What's your velocity? We all need to know what pace works best for us. When we exceed it, we start to experience burnout. When we don't even approach it, we experience boredom or depression. The key for all of us is to identify and stay within our zone.

Often when I give a speech the sound technician will ask me to speak into the microphone so that he can get a "sound level." He wants to determine what intensity of sound will work best in this room with this sound system and this speaker. Personal velocity is similar to this. Imagine the sound gauge on an audio recorder, the needle in a window that reacts to sounds. When you make a loud noise, the needle goes way up the dial to the right; when the noise level drops off, the needle goes back toward the left. That's kind of like velocity. If velocity were on a readable scale like that, you'd find an optimum range on that gauge where each person is at his or her best. And your range might be different from mine. Mine would be very high, someone else's might be even higher, and someone else's still higher.

It's different for all people. My son's velocity is fairly low, but there are a lot of people with lower velocity than his. My wife's velocity is moderate. There are people on both sides of her who would still be considered of moderate velocity.

So think about your own natural velocity. What zone are you comfortable in? Ever hear people talk about "the zone"? That's when you flow, you feel like you're in the groove, you know you're working at your best, you're at your right pace and level of intensity, the challenge you've bitten off is just about the size you can chew, and you know you're going after something you can handle.

When you get above your zone, when you're pushing yourself too hard, the first thing you experience is stress, a feeling of tension. Now, realize that stress can be a good thing. Stress is just pressure, resistance. When people handle this pressure in unhealthful ways, stress gets a negative connotation. If you continue to push harder against the pressure of stress, and if you stay anxious, you can start losing effectiveness.

Another thing you can experience if you keep on pushing harder is burnout, where you just feel, *What's the use?* You start losing motivation and need a time of recovery to get back into your zone.

On the lower side, if you don't push yourself hard enough, if you don't take on a big enough challenge, the first thing you experience is boredom. You're saying, with a long, drawn-out sigh, "This just doesn't feel like enough." It's not enough to keep you alert, awake, at your best, in your zone. You'll find that you become disinterested or bored if you continue without experiencing enough challenge to get yourself going. And boredom can become apathy, a total lack of interest.

Apathy leads to depression. In each case—boredom, apathy, and depression, or stress, anxiety, and burnout—the problem is that you are outside your natural velocity.

Mihaly Csikszentmihalyi, the author of *Flow: The Psychology of Optimal Experience,* studied the subject of peak performance and happiness: When are we happiest? When do we feel we've achieved something? What he found was that *we are happiest, we are in our zone, when we are challenged to achieve a goal.*

No, you cannot be in the zone when you're channel surfing and you're "challenged" to find the most interesting program on television! Challenge is at the core of our happiness. Now, you might say that challenge is stressful. Yes, it can be, but if you know what your natural velocity is, challenge can be fun.

You see, once you know what your best velocity is, you can stay in the zone almost all the time. We need to get out of the mentality of thinking, *What is my maximum, the most I could do?* and start asking, *What is my optimum, the best I can do?* You don't want to burn yourself out. You want to find your cruising speed so you can stay there all day long.

Velocity is a combination of energy and drive, combining physical and mental. Your natural range of physical energy is enhanced or limited by your nutrition, fitness, the amount of rest you get, the way you manage stress, and your attitude. You also have a natural degree of drive or self-motivation. Drive is affected by your self-esteem, the clarity of your purpose and goals, your awareness of possibilities, the appeal that your goals have to you, and your ability effectively to plan and follow that plan.

Here's a way to describe high, moderate, and low velocity in terms of energy and drive.

High velocity. Your drive is to be self-motivated. You love to work toward goals, particularly challenging goals. You have high aspirations and hold yourself and others to high standards. Competition excites you, and you have high expectations of yourself.

Your energy is allocated by always thinking about tasks, goals, or work interests. You even use leisure time to advance toward goals, whether they're personal or professional. You find inactivity to be frustrating. You prefer long hours filled with varied activity.

Moderate velocity. Your drive is to be somewhat self-motivated. You set reachable goals, have moderate aspirations, don't demand perfection, and accept competition, though you do not require it.

You allocate your energy with a balance of work and leisure. You prefer standard workdays that do not require constant overtime, with a moderate mix of activities. You use leisure time to complete chores and to socialize. You find inactivity relaxing, meaning you can just lie on the beach and feel good about the time spent.

Low velocity. You are driven primarily by immediate needs or by others. You find work generally demotivating. You prefer to work as a team player rather than be a solo performer or leader of the team. You'd prefer that someone else took the lead. You seldom set big goals. You have mild aspirations, not lofty ones. You really don't like competition, avoiding it if possible.

You use your energy to take things as they come. You are casual about your leisure time, which you use to pursue personal or social interests. You enjoy occasional inactivity and appreciate your own downtime.

Which pattern describes you the most? One way to identify your velocity is to look back over your life and see if it tends to reflect a higher or lower pattern of energy or drive. On the next page are some questions to help you.

There's no specific answer to any one of those questions that says, "This is high and this is low velocity," but there's a pattern in there that's easily identifiable.

Look back over the questions if you need to and just think about what your responses were. See whether they add up to a higher, a more moderate, or a lower form of intensity.

Remember, everyone has a pace and an intensity for which he or she is naturally suited. When you acknowledge that and attain your zone, you're at your best, your creativity increases, your productivity grows, and your peace of mind flourishes. You can indeed achieve that flow of energy, so start today to explore your velocity and find your optimum zone.

- Does your life look more achievement-oriented or more relationship-oriented?
- Have your achievements come at a faster or a slower pace than those of your peers?
- Is it important to you to be the first or the best?
- In school were you involved in lots of extracurricular activities or just a few?
- Are you happier working on projects or just hanging out with friends?
- Do you make and keep New Year's resolutions?
- Do you tend to be patient, or do you want things to happen right now?
- Have you accomplished most of the objectives you've set your mind to, or do you tend occasionally to lower your goals?
- How challenging are your goals? Do you want to change the world or just do your part?
- What kind of standards do you set for yourself? Do you drive to be the best in the entire world, or are you happy to be just playing the game?
- How long do you persist on a task before letting up?
- How much sleep do you need? Significantly more than seven or eight hours a night? Significantly less?
- Do you pack your day with activities, or do you kind of take things as they come?
- What would you do if you had loads of free time? Take on a new project or catch up on movies, reading, and visiting with friends?
- What do you do when you drive to work? Do you day-dream, listen to instructional tapes, or start talking to business associates on your car phone?
- On a long car trip, do you stop often to read historical markers or check out the sights, or do you make time straight for your destination? Why?
- What do you do between activities on vacation? Read, rest, or look for new adventures?

THOUGHT BREAK
Do you ever wish you had a different velocity? Why? How does your personal velocity currently affect your quality of life?

Ways to Stay at the Top of Your Zone

Several factors affect your performance. By controlling each of these you can stay at the top of your form, high in your zone of optimal velocity. The elements that make up your energy and drive are within your control to a large extent. By enhancing each of these, you increase your likelihood of staying at your optimum.

Energy Factors

Each person has a certain zone of energy that flows best when the following are nurtured: nutrition, strength, aerobic fitness, flexibility, rest, health, and repair. When you eat right and well, you have the fuel to be at your best. If you don't eat well, it's like running a Ferrari engine on regular old leaded gasoline. It may run, but it won't be race-ready. And the longer it runs on cheap fuel, the more likely it is to experience breakdown.

If you exercise regularly, your strength, circulation, flexibility, and vitality are at optimum. The American Council on Exercise has proved through numerous studies that illness, depression, aging, heart disease, and other problems are greatly reduced through regular exercise.

When you get ample rest, your body and mind replenish themselves and help you sustain high level performance. When you don't get enough rest, you cannot stay at your best. Retail tycoon John Wanamaker once said, "If you don't take time for rest and relaxation you will be forced sooner or later to make time for illness."

A body that is in good repair is more likely to be used fully than one that is not. Keith, a longtime friend of mine, once came to me for advice. His life was a mess and he needed some guidance. After we did a quick assessment of his personal priority wheel, it became obvious that one of his problems was physical. He had neglected his health and was eating poorly. He never exercised, he drank too often, and his teeth were in desperate need of repair. To avoid the discomfort and expense of a dental appointment, he simply learned to speak and smile without showing his teeth.

My advice to him was to get his teeth fixed immediately. He said, "Jim, you don't understand, my problems are mostly people problems and high stress. I need real help." I replied, "You don't understand. Every day you are reminded constantly of your neglect of your teeth. You can't eat or speak without thinking of it. If you don't fix your teeth, you will not feel you have made real improvement." He still protested but went to the dentist. Upon completion of the dental work, Keith was a changed man! He felt confident, healthier, and proud of himself for improving a part of his life. Sure, he had a lot of other things left to work on. *But by repairing one part of his body he regained the self-respect needed to go to work on the other parts of his life.* A body that is in good working order allows you to stay at the top of your zone. What parts of your body have you been neglecting lately?

Drive Factors

Things that affect your drive include: clarity of purpose, concentration, self-esteem, time management, organization, self-management, access to resources, and alignment. People who have worked to clarify what they want to do and why are more motivated to achieve. This is simply because their "motives" are more clear. Those who have learned how to manage their concentration skills are more able to sustain their focus. People who have high self-esteem tend to be more optimistic and tenacious in approaching their goals. With good time management and organization you can stay the course and use what energy you have even more efficiently. Self-management is the result of knowing yourself and mastering the skills of achievement. The greater your self-management, the more likely you are to act on your goals.

The easier it is for you to access information, tools, and assistance, the more likely you are to take action now instead of delaying. Think about the last time you procrastinated on something. If you had at your fingertips all that you needed in order to take action, wouldn't you have been less likely to delay action?

Alignment is the key to optimum velocity. If your physical needs and fitness are aligned with the demands you make on yourself, you stay in the zone. If not, you are less than your best. If your resource needs are met, you do better. If your relationships are highly functional and in alignment, you do a better job. So pay attention to these items and make their enhancement a daily priority. Just keep on making little improvements in each area in a natural ongoing way, and the cumulative effect will be optimum velocity. You will be at the top of your zone, and that is always your best place to be.

7. How Are You Smart? Multiple Intelligences in You

Several years ago actors Dustin Hoffman and Tom Cruise starred in the movie *Rain Man*. Maybe you saw it and remember that Raymond (the Rain Man) was a very unusual person. Because of his unusual mental state he couldn't carry on a normal conversation, and he couldn't focus, but when a box of toothpicks spilled over, Raymond could instantaneously count exactly how many toothpicks were on the floor. Instantaneously! Raymond could memorize all the phone numbers in a phone book. It was amazing! Raymond's mind was phenomenal.

The movie *Rain Man* was based on fact. Those like Raymond are classified technically as "autistic savants." That means he was literally a genius, a savant, a very learned person, and an autistic, a person who could not respond to outside stimuli. Raymond's greatest ability was mathematical; he could count and calculate as fast as a computer. But at the same time, he was dysfunctional interpersonally. So he was very intelligent yet unable to hold a conversation.

Considering Raymond's very high, computerlike mathematics ability tempered by his lack of communication skills, how *smart* do you think he was?

To be smart used to mean that you could score high on an IQ test or ace the Scholastic Aptitude Test. Smart people were the ones who were stars at math and spelling and had great memories. In many schools, kids were separated by their scores, with the higher-scoring kids getting more attention and more privileges than the lower-scoring ones.

In business, we've traditionally defined smart as the ability to solve problems and understand things quickly. In fact, quickness has been identified and accepted as a trait of intellect. Yet many of the world's great discoveries came not through quickness but through sustained, laborious thinking and creativity. Thomas Edison is said to have been a drudge despite his invention of the lightbulb. He reportedly tried thousands of times to create it with no success; it wasn't done quickly.

But many of our beliefs about intelligence have been shaken up recently. Foremost among the tree shakers has been Dr. Howard Gardner, whose book *Frames of Mind* cites seven types of intelligence. He says we've been measuring intelligence too narrowly.

Dr. Thomas Armstrong extends this concept in his book *Seven Kinds of Smart*. These great thinkers have proposed a much healthier question regarding intellect: not "Are you smart?" but "*How* are you smart?"

If we ask, "How is Raymond smart?" the answer is obvious: He's smart mathematically. That answer would give us a sense of what he would do well, what he would probably enjoy most, and where his greatest contribution would come from. Both Gardner and Armstrong have provided us with some valuable new insight. The essence of their conclusion is that there are at least seven intellects, all of which are possessed by everyone in different proportions. Your main smarts may be my lesser ones and vice versa.

Categories

If you were to go into a supermarket with a ten-item shopping list, and you found that every item on the shelves was stocked at random, you'd have peas on one shelf right next to frozen food, right next to meat, right next to garden supplies. Dog food would be in the cola section over by the bread and the . . . who knows? Even if you had only ten items on your list, how long would it take you to do your shopping? I believe it could take all day, maybe even longer depending on luck and on the size of the store.

What if, on the other hand, you went into the same super-market with a fifty-item shopping list—but the entire store was categorized in major groupings so that you had all the frozen food in one section, all the soft drinks in another section, all the vegetables in another section, all the meats in another. How long would it take you to find everything on your fifty-item shopping list? Not very long at all; you'd probably be out of there in an hour, assuming the checkout line wasn't too long or slow.

Now what's the difference? In the first case you had ten items on your shopping list and it would take you all day, and in the second scenario you had fifty items, five times the work to accomplish, and you could do it in one twenty-fourth of the time, one hour. The difference was the organization by *categories*. When things are arranged by category in your life, in your mind, in your work, even in your relationships, then it's much easier for you to understand them, locate things, and deal with them more effectively.

Here are Gardner's original seven intelligences, a way you can organize intellect or mental abilities by category so you can better understand your nature.

1. **Verbal intelligence. Word smart.** Related to words and language, the ability to think and communicate in verbal terms.

2. **Visual intelligence. Picture smart.** Relies on the sense of sight and/or the capacity to visualize; the ability to think in terms of shapes and arrangements of things, to see symbols and visualize possibilities.

3. **Physical intelligence. Body smart.** Relates to physical movement; the ability to "think" with your body, to understand things via physical involvement with them; hands-on knowing.

4. **Musical intelligence. Music smart.** Based on one's ability to recognize tonal patterns and think musically to know instinctively where a musical piece is going next, to use sounds and timing to express your thoughts eloquently.

5. **Mathematical and logical intelligence. Logic smart.**
   Sometimes thought to be scientific intelligence, this deals
   with powers of reasoning and how well we can relate to
   numbers, thinking in formulas, and systems.
6. **Interpersonal intelligence. People smart.** Deals with
   our person-to-person relationships, high empathy reveals
   this intellect, knowing how to relate well to all types of
   people.
7. **Intrapersonal intelligence. Self smart.** Relates to our
   ability to look inward and understand ourselves, the understanding of feelings and concepts, a strong sense of self.

What's so important about multiple intelligences? Our nature is
to use one or two smarts more frequently than the others. When
we use them, we develop a strength that Gardner and Armstrong
believe translates into our unique intelligence, sort of like our
trademark. Understanding multiple intelligences is a way to understand our nature more fully. In this book, we are spending
time with multiple intelligence so you can do three things: (1)
you can awaken your nature; (2) if you've not been using your
multiple intelligences fully, you can learn how to strengthen
more of them; and (3) you can learn how you can apply your
special multiple intelligences better in your daily life.

Here's a more in-depth look at each intelligence. Read each
description and see which ones apply to you.

Verbal intelligence means you have word smarts. Words are
your tools. You're good at explaining things or telling stories.
You might debate just for the heck of it. You are probably good
at games like Scrabble, where you make up words and can show
off your large vocabulary. You read lots of books, newspapers,
magazines, or reports (notice that stack of books next to your
desk or bed). Your friends often groan at your use of puns.

You can encourage your verbal intelligence by reading more,
consciously playing at expanding your vocabulary with a new
word of the week. You'd have fun with that. Look for new ways

to restate ideas. Some other ideas would be to challenge yourself with riddles or join a public speaking group like Toastmasters.

After you've awakened verbal intelligence, integrate it into your daily life by keeping a journal and writing down your daily story, or try your hand at poetry. Honor that nature by paying attention to it, by nurturing it.

Visual intelligence is in the realm of pictures, patterns, and designs. If you have strong visual intelligence, you probably draw out your ideas on paper. You creatively see things from different angles. You find it easy to visualize something even without a physical image to assist you. As a kid, you loved to lie on the grass and watch the clouds move across the sky because you could see shapes in the clouds. Look! There's a horse! There's Mickey Mouse!

You probably like to doodle or draw; in fact, in a meeting you probably have to use the white board to draw out the situation or problem so everyone can better understand it. You also like to use charts and symbols to get your point across. And—one last trait—you always have a pencil or pen handy.

If you'd like to encourage your natural visual intelligence, learn to MindMap. Have you heard that term before? Tony Buzan started MindMapping back in the eighties. MindMapping is a process for note taking, brainstorming, or planning projects that uses drawing, color, and pictures graphically and creatively to capture ideas. There are many books on MindMapping techniques; the best I have found is appropriately titled *MindMapping* and it is written by my friend Joyce Wycoff, founder of the Innovation Network.

To sharpen visual intelligence, assemble puzzles, play Pictionary, or do mazes. Another technique would be to draw diagrams and flowcharts of all your processes. Or if you've always wanted to take an art class, make the time.

To integrate your visual intelligence into your daily life, offer to be the note taker or scribe at the next team meeting or the secretary at your volunteer board meeting but add illustrations to the notes (get permission beforehand if the meeting is important). Use your ability to draw as often as possible. Acknowledge your visual skill and hone it.

If you have high **physical or body intelligence,** you're probably good at sports; you're very well coordinated. You might even be a gymnast. As a kid, you enjoyed phys ed class and got good PE grades. Or your intellect may show up less obviously in work with your hands, art, sculpture, tinkering, gardening, model building.

You have a natural ability to dance and know how to express yourself well with your body—you and comedian Jim Carrey! Others might tell you that you walk with confidence. You pick up new actions easily. After years of not playing billiards or darts, you can enter a game and quickly recapture your skills.

To sharpen body intelligence, do anything that requires hands-on learning. While people of greater visual intelligence can picture an idea to learn, or those with greater verbal intelligence can listen to a tape to learn, people with predominant body intelligence need to do to learn. And they will learn exceptionally well if they can involve the body at the same time. They are likely to be physical learners in other ways too. They may recall things best when they are anchored to a feeling or movement.

Another way to encourage body intelligence is to get involved in the arts such as by joining a dance group. You can express yourself very well through movement. You're probably good at charades. To maximize your body intelligence in daily life, acknowledge your need for physical movement. Get up often and move around. Make time to exercise every day. You need it to be your best.

While **musical intelligence** does focus on music, rhythm, resonance, and vibration, it also extends to sounds from nature, such as birds, or water cascading down a waterfall, or the tone of a human voice. Have you ever been annoyed merely by someone's voice? Maybe the laugh of someone with a strong nasal quality to the voice?

If you have strong musical intelligence, you probably are

noticing the sound of the voice in your head as you read. A game you like is the old television program *Name That Tune.* "I can name that tune in four notes!" Well, sure you can!

If you have greater musical intelligence, you probably hum, whistle, or sing, maybe even when you're not aware of it. No doubt you love musicals and rhythm performances.

Do you know that we are all born with a biological awareness of rhythm and music? It's true. Studies with infants prove that when three-month-old babies hear pleasant, smooth music, they play calmly. But when the music switches to a discordant, uneven melody, babies become cranky, irritable, and fidgety. Humans like even melodies. Scientists don't understand why our brain responds so early to music, but it is a fact that it does.

You probably learned the alphabet by singing the alphabet song. You might play a musical instrument or sing in a choir, barbershop quartet, or a Sweet Adeline's group. You like to go to concerts of any kind. And your personal stereo system is one of your prized possessions. What a collection of CDs you have!

To encourage your musical intelligence, broaden your appreciation of all kinds of music. Change the radio station every now and then to see what else is out there. If you haven't played an instrument in a while, pick it up again. Or add music to your exercise routine. You will especially respond to using music to reduce stress because it's your natural intelligence.

You probably have more opportunity to integrate musical intelligence into your daily life than you think. Sounds are around us everywhere. Use your sharp listening skills when in a conversation. Stop and listen to all the sounds around you. Turn off the radio and just listen to the sounds outside the window. Appreciate all the sounds in nature.

Mathematical or logical intelligence has to do with numbers and geometric designs, and it also has to do with problem solving and analysis. Unlike musical intelligence, which is displayed with making music or being in direct contact with a musical sound, math/logic intelligence is best expressed when you're faced with a new challenge.

If you have strong math/logic intelligence, math or science probably was your best class in school. You prefer strategy games like chess. You love logic puzzles. Mysteries and problem-solving discussions intrigue you. You might even have that old Rubik's cube around on a shelf somewhere. I'll bet you have a computer at home and may even know how to program it. You are very curious and love to search for proof instead of just taking anything at face value.

To encourage math/logic intelligence, search for patterns in everything, whether it's constellations in the sky, how music is repeated in a song, or how history repeats itself. You have a special talent for analyzing and classifying. Another way to sharpen your math smarts is to put away the calculator and calculate numbers in your head. You can do it—and you love the challenge.

Apply math/logic intelligence in your daily life as a matter of awareness. Your nature is to be logical, to understand abstract patterns. The value you bring is your ability to see the logic, or the lack of it. Think of Mr. Spock, the half-Vulcan first officer in *Star Trek*. Vulcans were the masters of logic. Spock lacked high interpersonal intelligence, but no one could argue with his logic!

Interpersonal intelligence is people smarts. If you have high interpersonal intelligence, you are an excellent communicator. You love to socialize with any and all kinds of different people. You like any game where you can talk or team with others. You hate to be left out of anything! You love when people come to you for advice because you always have a sympathetic ear.

To encourage interpersonal intelligence, join a team, get active with people of different backgrounds or thinking styles. You might enjoy volunteer work or taking an improvisation acting class. You're very good at sensing what to do with other people on the spot. Somehow you seem to know what to say to most people. You easily open new conversations.

I once attended a celebration of the anniversary of the filming of the movie *Some Like It Hot* at the Hotel Del Coronado in San Diego, California. When we met some of the movie stars, I didn't have much to say. I wanted to contribute to the conversation, but I couldn't think of anything interesting to say. But my wife, Paula, spoke easily to all of them. She struck up conversations about their kids, joked with them, and so forth. I was impressed with how her interpersonal intellect worked for her.

In your daily life, you may be so busy speaking that you haven't fully developed listening. To really master being a people person, you need to slow down and be aware of other people's opinions and feelings. This will make your interpersonal intelligence even stronger.

Intrapersonal intelligence is the ability to look inside and know yourself. We can also call this self smarts. A person of high intrapersonal intelligence is uniquely aware of self and probably comfortable with what he or she sees. If you are like this, you might seem to be a loner because you prefer to work alone. You can focus and concentrate better that way. You are fascinated by feelings, philosophies, thought patterns, and such internal experiences. You enjoy observing yourself and the reactions of others.

Intrapersonals are the least team-oriented people. Though they may work well on a team, they are equally effective on their own. My intrapersonal intellect is one of my most developed. One way I know this is by observing that for years I have exercised alone rather than joining others in a group activity. I love the solitude and ability to contemplate while exercising. My wife, on the other hand, insists on exercising with others. For her it is a social activity. If you have strong intrapersonal intelligence, you are used to focusing on your own goals, goals that are meaningful to you, not waiting to find out what the team goal is. You are very well aware of your strengths and weaknesses.

To encourage your natural intrapersonal intelligence, raise your self-awareness by stopping to observe what you feel at any one moment. Notice when your mood changes. Another way to awaken and strengthen the intrapersonal is to check in with your personal goals. Make time on a weekly or monthly basis to see if you are actively pursuing them. If you are working on them, you probably feel better about yourself. One more strategy would be to make time every day for silent reflection. Think through a project you just finished. Intrapersonals have the skill to reflect from all angles, to analyze and assimilate the learning.

Now that we've reviewed each of these intelligences in detail, you may be thinking, *Jim, this is all very interesting, and I see how this can help me personally, but does it have any business applications? For instance, how can I take a team of people and get them all using their multiple intelligences in a team, like the people I work with?* Glad you asked!

Let's look at a situation where a team has to give a presentation. A good way to position team members based on their multiple intelligences would be first to make sure everyone is involved in the planning session. The verbal person would be great as the presenter and scriptwriter.

The visual person would be very good at putting together the slides, flip charts, or overheads, as well as determining the proper placement of people and things.

The math/logic person would be best putting the flowcharts, graphs, and statistics together into a logical sequence, making sense of the presentation, and helping others understand it accurately.

The intrapersonal individual could do the demonstration of how the product or service works conceptually and how people will think and feel about it. This person could help define how people will react to and analyze the information.

The body intelligence person could also be the presenter, but he is also into "feeling." So I'd probably have him build the set, select the feel of the paper of the handouts or workbooks, and choreograph the presentation.

The interpersonal person would make a great welcomer or introducer and would do well with facilitating the question-and-answer section.

Now you're probably wondering about that musical intelligence team member. What could she do? Examine the rhythm and flow of the presentation. Maybe even add sound effects. Creative ways to use a person's unique intelligence are all around you. Notice more.

Can you begin to see how understanding your own and others' multiple intelligence strengths can help you? The ways you are smart are part of the seed within you and they hold the key to your further growth. You can take pride in the special ways that you are smart and appreciate others for their special gifts.

You can develop all of your different types of intellect; you can become strong in every one of the seven. But chances are that a few of those seven will be natural strengths for you and the others will come more slowly. So learn to notice what kind of smarts you possess already. Start now to notice more and explore your natural intelligence.

THOUGHT BREAK
- Which of the seven intelligences do you most identify with?
- Think of someone close to you, your spouse or partner, a parent, a child. What do you think his or her strongest intelligences are?
- Is that intelligence different from yours?
- If so, do you have a hard time communicating or connecting with him or her?
- Can you see his or her special gift?

Everyone has all seven intellects. The key to using them is to notice their existence and the part they play in daily life, then cultivate each of them. Your growth will be natural and automatic.

8. Exploring How You Think: What Is Your Intellectual Bandwidth?

Intelligence, intellect, smarts—or whatever you call it— seems to be an aspect of human existence that is noticeable and, in some cases, measurable, as with the IQ test. Smarts seem to catch our attention.

But what exactly does it mean to be intelligent, to be smart? In 1921, Louis Terman defined intelligence as *the ability to carry on abstract thinking.* Herbert Woodrow called it *the capacity to acquire capacity.* S. S. Colvin said that people *possess intelligence insofar as they have learned or can learn to adjust themselves to their environment.*

In his book *The Triarchic Mind,* Robert Sternberg defined intellect *as the ability to learn and use information to shape or adapt to our circumstances.* I like that: the ability to learn, which means we build on information to shape or adapt our circumstances. Since humans are the only animals to participate in and actively control the shaping of their environment, intellect is our unique talent. Regardless of whether we are talking about logical intellect or physical or musical or even intrapersonal, Sternberg's definition applies.

Let's look at learning as the first factor of intelligence. For example, when you pick up a television's remote control for the first time, it may be so complex as to seem unlearnable. But then you identify the on/off button, then the volume control, then the channel selector, and so on. And each one you "get" increases your TV remote "vocabulary" and helps you understand the other functions.

Another way to define intellect is *the ability to make distinctions.* Distinguishing among all those buttons on the remote is what allows you to use them properly.

Have you ever looked at the cockpit of a commercial aircraft? If all you see is a bunch of dials and switches, you'll never fly the plane. There are so many gauges and instruments that it seems it would require a genius just to use them (maybe it does). But you and I have the capacity literally to become more intelligent when we recognize more distinctions. Once we learn the patterns among the gauges and see that all of the gauges on the left are of a certain type and those on the right all perform the same central function, then this vast information settles into categories or into a system. And the next thing you know you can understand how to fly the plane.

Every time you learn something new, there is literally, physically, an increase in the neural connections within the neocortex of your brain. So when it learns something new, your brain is capable of learning even more new things than before. You physically have more connections with which you can access memories or solutions. If you want to have higher intellect, you need to see more distinctions. *To know more, notice more.*

In any situation, the more facets of it you notice, the more distinctions you make between the elements. The more possibilities you see, the more options you have before you.

Here's another example: The famous cliff divers of Acapulco are daredevils who climb a sheer cliff several stories high and then dive into the turbulent surf below. If they were to time their dive wrong, the surf would be out when they hit the water, and they would break their necks and die.

When they get it right, they recover and swim ashore to dive another day. As these divers stand on the cliff, seemingly trying to muster the courage to dive, what they're actually doing is watching the surf, noticing the timing of the waves. They concentrate on the nature of the water. They get in tune with the difference, the distinctions between the ebb and the flow.

They can be intelligent about the dive because they've learned to make distinctions most people wouldn't notice. In any situation, if you train yourself to make more distinctions, to notice more, then you'll increase your alternatives and chances for success; you will literally become *more intelligent* in dealing with it.

Once you've made distinctions, what can greater intellect do for you? In *The Triarchic Mind,* Sternberg said we use our intellect in three primary ways: to adapt to our circumstances, to select better circumstances, or to shape our circumstances as we desire.

So we use our smarts to adapt, select, and shape.

Adapting means we adjust to a new or changed circumstance. For instance, if you are attempting to cross a freeway on foot (not a recommended activity), you may adapt by standing on the curb until traffic clears. You won't make any progress in this mode, but you will be ready when the opportunity presents itself. To *select* is to choose in accordance with your preference. If you prefer to advance across the freeway faster, you may select certain spots where there are gaps in traffic and run temporarily to those spots. You are still at the mercy of the traffic, but you are managing your responses more actively. Your other choice is to *shape* the situation, to give it a form you find pleasing, to define the parameters. To shape the traffic you could create a stop sign or a detour to clear a path for yourself.

In other words, adapting is accepting the circumstances as they are. You maintain your original course. You compromise by adjusting a little bit in order to maintain the status quo. You might find yourself adapting when you get a new boss. At first you're not sure how he or she will support you or manage you. So you adapt to the change by watching, waiting to see what the new boss wants, and then adjusting your performance and behavior to meet your new boss's preferences or criteria. In adapting we don't seek new options.

On the other hand, selecting involves analyzing the circumstances more thoroughly so you can select the preferred response or action. To select we need to seek new options. With a new boss you could select how and when to interact with her based on the best times in her day or her preferred supervisory style. To shape the situation you could meet with your boss to redefine your job and take on different responsibilities. (I once did this after reading a book on managing people. I met with my boss and showed him how to manage me differently in order to get even better performance from me.) Here is another example: When we gain weight, we might adapt by buying clothes a size larger. Or we could lose those extra pounds by selecting foods lower in calories. When faced with the numbers on the scale getting higher, someone who wanted to shape the situation would look at the big picture (no pun intended) and decide what kind of body he wanted, what level of health he wanted, and then develop a lifestyle, nutrition, and exercise plan to achieve it.

Each of these abilities can be developed: adapt, select, shape.

Thinking Styles: Your Intellectual Bandwidth

Another way of looking at these actions is to examine our correlated thinking styles: operational, strategic, and conceptual. Thinking style is not intellect; it is the way you *use* your intellect. We all have our own distinctive, natural style of thinking, which defines how we apply our intellect to most situations. Some people deal first with the concepts, others look first for the strategies or alternatives available to them, and still others look first at the functions or operations.

Another way of describing this is to use the computer community's term *bandwidth*. Bandwidth describes how much information a computer can efficiently process at one time. A computer that can do ten calculations at the same time has a greater bandwidth than a computer that does only three at once.

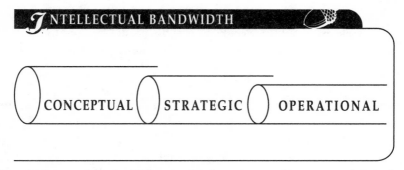

People have a bandwidth too. And you can observe one's bandwidth with relative ease. Just start noticing how much information someone can process efficiently at one time.

Around 80 percent of the people you meet tend to think operationally, about 18 percent of the people tend to be strategic thinkers, and only about 2 percent are conceptual thinkers. Again, operational thinkers *adapt* to the situation; they see what is and they adapt to it. Operational thinkers prefer to deal with one thing at a time. They are most efficient when they can focus on each item separately. Strategic thinkers tend to *select* the situations they want out of the many alternatives they've identified. Strategic thinkers are always looking at options and possibilities. They process several ideas at once and consider the relative value of each alternative. And the conceptuals see the whole thing in a much larger context and look to how they can *shape* the future. Conceptual thinkers have a huge bandwidth. They see relationships between everything.

Here's a closer look: Some people see everything on the practical or functional level. What it is, what it does, that's the operational. The strategic see everything on the level of how it could be used, what effect it would have on other things. And then a small group are the conceptuals who see everything in the context of what it means, how it relates to the rest of the world.

- An operational thinker might pick up a pencil and start experimenting with it to see how it writes.
- A strategic thinker would start exploring the many ways the pencil could be used.

- A conceptual thinker would reflect on how something as simple as a piece of wood and graphite could be used to advance humankind through written language and symbols.

Now imagine these three people working as a project team to plan the relocation of their company's headquarters to a large neighboring city. Where the operational might be very concerned about where to put all the desks, the conceptual would literally be contemplating the potential impact of not using desks at all in the future. Strategic thinkers might serve as good translators between the two, but their differences would lead to much disagreement until they learned to value and respect the operating levels of each other's thinking, their style. All these things matter, but they should be considered one level at a time, starting with the concept, then the strategies, and then the operations. The more likely and maybe more productive team would include a variety of operationals, a few strategics, and very few conceptuals. Fortunately, that's about how the population's distributed.

- The operational thinker would be looking at where the building would be, whether the machines and equipment would fit in it, what would go where, where the people would park, how it would feel to work in the new location.
- The strategic thinker would be thinking about the transportation needs, closeness to suppliers, time required for the transition from the old building to the new one, impact on the morale and the productivity of the people, operations costs, and the new opportunities that were being created.
- The conceptual thinker would see thousands of possibilities in this move and would wonder what kind of message this move sends to customers, stockholders, and competitors. He or she would also think about the long-term implications of the move, available labor pool now and in the future, population changes, future changes in technology, and the psychological impact of all this on those who work there.

Which of these styles is most natural to you? By the way, before you get hung up on judgment here, a lot of people might say, "Well, hey, wait a minute! The conceptuals are more intelligent, they're smarter than the strategics. And the strategics are smarter than the operationals. Therefore, being operational is the least desirable of the three, right?" No, I don't think so!

The way it works is: Most of the functions that need to be performed in this world are operational. On a personal level, there's everything from brushing your teeth to preparing food, getting the job done in almost any case. Only a small proportion of the work that needs to be done in life is strategic work. And an even smaller proportion is conceptual work. There's a place for all three styles, and everyone needs to have some working familiarity with each of them. But that won't change your nature; you still have a natural thinking style that is the one most comfortable for you, which determines what types of activities you're drawn toward and feel most comfortable with. So which style is most natural to you? Each has its place, and none is better or worse; there's a need for all three.

By the way, there's a big range of difference even within the styles. There are conceptuals who are good idea people, and then there are conceptuals such as Albert Einstein or Buckminster Fuller who are some of the great minds throughout history. Strategic thinkers include everyone from top negotiators to architects and teachers who translate other people's ideas into useful applications. Operational thinkers range from someone like actor John Wayne to some of the world's best parents, technicians, athletes, carpenters, and cooks. But you'll also find conceptual actors, strategic cooks, and operational entrepreneurs and inventors. There's room for everybody.

Ways You Can Observe and Grow Your Intellect

Independent of your thinking style, you can observe and increase your bandwidth somewhat by developing the elements that make up your intellect. I've identified eight indicators of bandwidth that apply to all people, and all eight can be developed. These are the ways one's intellect is expressed or revealed. You can use these to observe the intellectual abilities and the thinking styles of people, and you can work on each of these to increase your intellectual possibilities.

8 INDICATORS OF BANDWIDTH

1. **Ability to Make Distinctions**
2. **A Wide Vocabulary**
3. **The Use of Metaphors and Analogies**
4. **Flexibility and Adaptiveness**
5. **Problem Solving**
6. **Time Orientation**
7. **Sensitivity**
8. **Memory**

1. The Ability to Make Distinctions

The more you are able to notice, the more you are able to know. The more you know, the more options you've created for yourself. Start now to expand your awareness, noticing more, by completing this exercise: Imagine that you are a reporter who must accurately describe every aspect of a situation to others later on. Notice what you see, feel, hear, smell, taste, and otherwise experience. Notice the patterns that are present. Look at the floor covering: How many colors and textures do you see? Notice the sounds: Where are they coming from? Are they pleasant or irritating? Notice the other people present: What are they doing? What do you notice about them?

2. A Wide Vocabulary

This is not a vocabulary that just comes straight out of an encyclopedia or a dictionary, but the vocabulary that applies to the world you live in, the things you work with, the people you connect to, the society in which you live, the culture in which you operate. In how many ways can you describe and explain what you know, see, and experience? For example, motorcycling has its own vernacular, as do all sports. There are words to describe the different types of bikes: sport, standard, touring, dual-sport, cruiser, trials, dirt, and custom. All have their own meanings and subgroups. Then there are the accessories: fairings, sissy bars, brake calipers, tankbags, floorboards, pegs, bar-end weights. It is a world with its own jargon. So is boating, football, fashion design, cooking, taxi driving, and so forth. The wider your vocabulary is within each context, the more intelligently you can communicate and comprehend actions and ideas. You'll see more options, and you'll have more ways to remember things and more ways to communicate those things to other people. So constantly learn new words, new meanings.

3. The Use of Metaphors and Analogies

The more a person can speak naturally in symbols and stories, the more information he or she can convey in a short time. All of the great teachers throughout history have been storytellers, and the people who have made the most vivid impressions on us in speeches or in writing have been those who created vivid images of their messages—brilliant pictures and moving similes to bring home a point. The acorn story is a metaphor for personal growth. It compares the acorn's ability to grow only into an oak to the innate and *unique* potential in every person. What metaphors or analogies can you adopt to create greater understanding of your relationships, your work, your passions—your life?

4. Flexibility and Adaptiveness

The more options you see, the more flexible you'll be. The more you understand the uniqueness and the individuality of each person, the less you'll judge people and the more you can adapt to them. If you tend to insist on approaching life in the same ways day after day, you diminish your intellectual ability. Intellect thrives on variety and new information. Seek new ways, listen to people you'd typically ignore, travel different paths, read different magazines, go to different movies than you normally would. Cultivate your ability to be flexible.

5. Problem Solving

You can improve your problem-solving skills by learning certain systems, methods, and formulas for problem solving— everything from creative thinking techniques to systematic checklists that you can use in solving the problem. An excellent model I had the opportunity to collaborate on is in the book *Yes or No* by Spencer Johnson, M.D. He divides decision making into two primary parts: practical and personal. First he guides you through the "head" side of the equation using logic and analysis, then he leads you into the "heart" part of the decision. Questions such as "How do I really feel about this?" and "Am I telling myself the truth?" reveal essential elements often overlooked in traditional problem solving.

6. Time Orientation

You can distinguish among the conceptuals, strategics, and operationals by observing how they relate with time. Operationals tend to be a little nostalgic, reflecting on the past and viewing the current reality as their main context or frame of reference. Strategics look at the present as it relates to the immediate future; they are always looking for alternatives and thinking about possibilities. Conceptuals, on the other hand, seem to be living in the day after tomorrow or year after next. They're always projecting their minds way beyond their current reality and thinking about the further implications or the broader concepts behind things. Learn to shift your time frame while thinking about things, and you will broaden your intellectual possibilities. If you're generally a conceptual thinker, try switching time frames with the operational or strategic styles. If you're primarily strategic, try thinking conceptually or operationally about time. And if you're generally oriented to time as an operational, switch gears to conceptual or strategic every now and then.

7. Sensitivity

The more you notice, the more distinctions you make, the more sensitive you'll become to other people. If I notice only that you're being resistant to what I'm trying to get you to do, then my response to that is probably going to be defensive or aggressive; I'll just try harder to get you to do what I want you to do. But if I can be more sensitive to *why* you're not doing it, what your motive is for resisting, what you fear or what you are hoping to accomplish, my whole approach would change. The more I understand you, the less aggressive I'll tend to be and the more effective I'll be in finding a better way to relate. Study individual differences, take a course in personality types, practice empathy, and you will become more sensitive to others. Reading this book is a sensitivity enhancer.

8. Memory

The more you remember, the more alternatives you'll have. The more you remember, the more ways you can recall and use information strategically to your desired outcome. In a given situation, the person who remembers the most of what he or she needs to know will be the one who acts most intelligently to achieve the desired outcomes. So work on your memory, develop your skills, sharpen the ability to retain and interrelate information. You will literally be more intelligent.

Have you noticed that just now you've become more intelligent about intelligence? You're making finer distinctions, you're noticing more, and you'll now see more ways to deal with intellect both in yourself and in others.

THOUGHT BREAK
- Do you think you're smart? Why? Why not?
- Would you like to change? How? Why?
- What's your natural bandwidth? Describe how you know that.
- How can you most easily improve your thinking ability?
- Where will you start?
- Think of someone you know or work with. Using the eight indicators of bandwidth as your guide, assess the overall bandwidth of that person.

9. Behavioral Style: What Others Call Your "Personality"

Throughout history, humans have attempted to explain the differences among them in a lot of different ways. The earliest recorded efforts were found in ancient astrology. Astrology said that the way the heavens were aligned when you were born determined your behavior. Astrologers used twelve constellations in the sky and four major groupings, symbolized by earth, air, fire, and water. And they said that the movement of the sun, moon, and planets at a certain time would influence your behavior patterns or your fate.

Thousands of years ago, the stars were all they had to go on.

Then about 400 B.C., Hippocrates, "the father of medicine," developed the concept of temperaments. He identified four basic temperaments: choleric, phlegmatic, sanguine, and melancholy. And he said that these were determined by the elements *in* your body, not the stars *outside* your body.

The key elements he identified as contributors to your temperament were blood, phlegm, black bile, and yellow bile. That might have been okay for Hippocrates with his medical background, but I don't talk about this theory in polite company very much, and certainly not over dinner.

Then, in 1923, Dr. Carl Jung wrote *Psychological Types,* in which he described sixteen types and then boiled them down to four major ones: the intuitor, the thinker, the feeler, and the sensor. Jung, like his predecessors, found the magic number of four types.

When it was published, Jung's book was the most scientific work that had been done on personality patterns to date. Since the early twenties, lots of people have developed models of personality type. The well-known Myers-Briggs Type Indicator is based on the work of Carl Jung. If you've been in the business community for very long, chances are you've gone to a seminar, heard a speech, or read an article about personality types that broke them down into four basic types. Now, it doesn't matter if you call the four types "sneezy," "dopey," "sleepy," and "doc"; there are still four basic types. Call them A, B, C, and D if you want to. The point is that there are different types that exist in everyone; you have all four, and I have all four. But *one* of those four is your dominant type.

Several years ago I developed a behavioral model with Dr. Tony Alessandra to express and explain communication differences, and we called it "relationship strategies for dealing with the differences in people." We were trying to take a variety of concepts on personality types and boil them down to one simple model that could be easily taught, understood, and used by almost anybody. We must have succeeded, because our six-cassette audio album, *Relationship Strategies,* went on to sell well over one hundred thousand copies and became one of the all time best-sellers for Nightingale-Conant Corporation.

Let me help you understand a basic concept of behavior. There are two elements of behavior. One of those is called openness, the degree to which someone readily shares feelings, thoughts, and responses. On one end of the scale is high openness. People who are highly open share their information and their feelings readily.

On the opposite end of the scale is low openness. These people don't usually speak up first and don't speak without a great deal of consideration. I call this "self-contained" behavior.

The other scale I call "directness." On one end of the scale

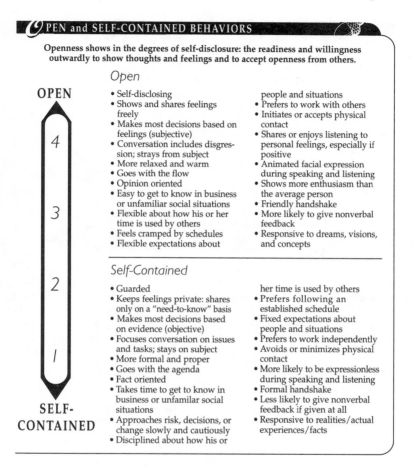

OPEN and SELF-CONTAINED BEHAVIORS

Openness shows in the degrees of self-disclosure: the readiness and willingness outwardly to show thoughts and feelings and to accept openness from others.

Open

OPEN

4

3

- Self-disclosing
- Shows and shares feelings freely
- Makes most decisions based on feelings (subjective)
- Conversation includes digression; strays from subject
- More relaxed and warm
- Goes with the flow
- Opinion oriented
- Easy to get to know in business or unfamiliar social situations
- Flexible about how his or her time is used by others
- Feels cramped by schedules
- Flexible expectations about

people and situations
- Prefers to work with others
- Initiates or accepts physical contact
- Shares or enjoys listening to personal feelings, especially if positive
- Animated facial expression during speaking and listening
- Shows more enthusiasm than the average person
- Friendly handshake
- More likely to give nonverbal feedback
- Responsive to dreams, visions, and concepts

Self-Contained

2

1

SELF-CONTAINED

- Guarded
- Keeps feelings private: shares only on a "need-to-know" basis
- Makes most decisions based on evidence (objective)
- Focuses conversation on issues and tasks; stays on subject
- More formal and proper
- Goes with the agenda
- Fact oriented
- Takes time to get to know in business or unfamilar social situations
- Approaches risk, decisions, or change slowly and cautiously
- Disciplined about how his or

her time is used by others
- Prefers following an established schedule
- Fixed expectations about people and situations
- Prefers to work independently
- Avoids or minimizes physical contact
- More likely to be expressionless during speaking and listening
- Formal handshake
- Less likely to give nonverbal feedback if given at all
- Responsive to realities/actual experiences/facts

you see people who are so direct that they're almost blunt. To make a point, they'd say exactly what's in their mind. They let you know where they stand on an issue, speak right up, and are not at all reluctant to take a position.

On the opposite side of the scale are the indirect people. Indirect people are a little more tactful. They are more cautious, waiting to see what develops before acting, or waiting to see where things are headed before becoming involved. They want to see how it goes first. Instead of appearing active, they appear passive.

DIRECT and INDIRECT BEHAVIORS

Indirect

- Approaches risk, decisions, or change slowly and cautiously
- Infrequent contributor to group conversations
- Infrequently uses gestures and voice intonation to emphasize points
- Often makes qualified statements: "According to my sources...," "I think so"
- Emphasizes points through explanation of the content of the message
- Questions tend to be for clarification, support, or information
- Reserves expression of opinions
- More patient and cooperative
- Diplomatic; collaborative
- When not in agreement (if it's no big deal), most likely to go along
- Understanding; reserved
- Initial eye contact is intermittent
- At social gatherings, more likely to wait for others to introduce themselves
- Gentle handshake
- Tends to follow established rules and policies

INDIRECT ◄ (**A**   **B**   **C**   **D**) ► DIRECT

Direct

- Approaches risk, decisions, or change quickly and spontaneously
- Frequent contributor to group conversations
- Frequently uses gestures and voice intonation to emphasize points
- Often makes emphatic statements: "This is so!" "I'm positive!"
- Emphasizes points through confident vocal intonation and assertive body language
- Questions tend to be rhetorical, to emphasize points or to challenge information
- Expresses opinions readily
- Less patient; competitive
- Confronting; controlling
- More likely to maintain position when not in agreement (argues)
- Intense; assertive
- Initial eye contact is sustained
- More likely to introduce self to others at social gathering
- Firm handshake
- Tends to bend and break established rules and policies

Think about yourself in those two respects, openness and directness. How open do you tend to be most of the time? Depending on the situation, sometimes you might be more open and sometimes you might be more self-contained. Of course you are, that's called *flexibility.* But think about the pattern. Where's home base for you? Where's your natural level? Are you naturally more open, outgoing, spontaneous, or naturally a little more reserved, a little more watchful? Note where your home is on this scale by choosing 1, 2, 3, or 4 to locate your normal pattern of openness.

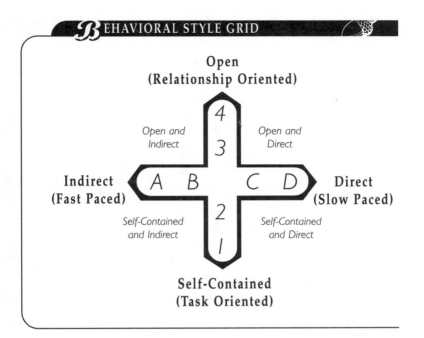

As you are thinking about your natural pattern, remember that there is no better or worse. It's equally okay to be anywhere on the scale. There is no right or wrong; there's just your nature, your natural pattern.

Now let's go to the directness scale. Imagine a horizontal line. Instead of numbers, we'll use the letters A, B, C, and D. Put the A on the left and the D on the right. The left-hand side of the directness scale would be low directness, behavior that is cautious or tactful. The right-hand side of the directness scale is highly direct, where someone speaks up readily, jumps right into things, tends to take charge.

Which side of that directness scale do you find your home base on? Do you find it on the indirect side or the direct side? On the indirect side would be A or B. A is the least direct, B is the next direct. On the right-hand side of the scale is directness, C or D. D is highly direct, C fairly high. Choose a letter to indicate your natural level of directness, your home base.

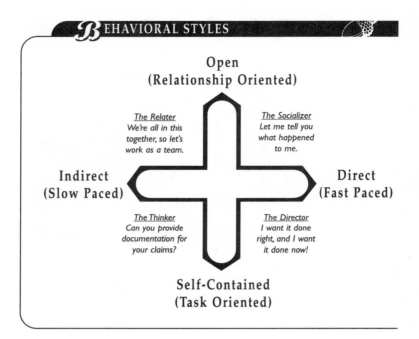

If you chose both a 1 or a 2 with an A or a B, then you are in the *lower left* corner of that grid; that quadrant is called the thinker behavioral style. The thinker pattern or behavioral style tends to be indirect and self-contained.

Did you choose the thinker pattern? Whom do you see on television or in the movies that might be a model of a thinker pattern? Whenever I see reruns of the science fiction show *Star Trek,* I see Spock, the first officer of the *Starship Enterprise,* as the most obvious thinker type. Spock had very high logic, definitely was detail oriented, did not suffer fools lightly, was systematic, and thought before he acted. Not at all like Captain Kirk, the director type, who would jump boldly into any situation, emotions flaring.

If you chose both a 1 or a 2 and a C or a D, then you'll be in the *lower right* corner of our grid, along with Mike Wallace, the

SUMMARY OF STYLES

RELATER

- Slow at taking action and making decisions
- Likes close, personal relationships
- Dislikes interpersonal conflict
- Supports and "actively" listens to others
- Weak at goal setting and self-direction
- Has excellent ability to gain support from others
- Works slowly and cohesively with others
- Seeks security and belongingness
- Good counseling skills

SOCIALIZER

- Spontaneous actions and decisions
- Likes involvement
- Dislikes being alone
- Exaggerates and generalizes
- Tends to dream and often gets others caught up in those dreams
- Jumps from one activity to another
- Works quickly and excitedly with others
- Seeks esteem and acknowledgment
- Good persuasive skills

THINKER

- Cautious actions and decisions
- Likes organization and structure
- Dislikes involvement
- Asks many questions about specific details
- Prefers objective, task-oriented, intellectual work environment
- Wants to be right, so can be overly reliant on data collection
- Works slowly and precisely alone
- Good problem-solving skills

DIRECTOR

- Decisive actions and decisions
- Likes control, dislikes inaction
- Prefers maximum freedom to manage self and others
- Cool, independent, and competitive
- Low tolerance for feelings, attitudes, and advice of others
- Works quickly and impressively alone
- Good administrative skills

in-your-face interviewer of TV's *60 Minutes.* That's the director quadrant, like a director on a movie set. The director is a take-charge type who measures things by outcomes, likes to get things done, and doesn't like to waste time doing a lot of talking. Directors move quickly and decisively.

If you chose both an A or a B and a 3 or a 4, then you're in the *upper left* corner of our grid. That's called the relater quadrant. The relater pattern or behavioral style relates most to connecting with other people. Relaters tend to be soft-spoken, which comes from their indirectness. They are easygoing and very people oriented (with their high openness they're naturally drawn to other people), love to be involved in discussions, like to build one-to-one relationships, and people tend to be the center of their work life and their home life. One of the best-loved relaters while in the national spotlight was First Lady Barbara Bush. Her warm and supportive style made everyone feel that she was part of their family.

If you chose both a 3 or a 4 and a C or a D, then your style is in the *upper right* corner of our grid, which is called the socializer quadrant. These are the people who are always socializing, always talking, always have something to say. You get on an elevator with a socializer, and even if you're total strangers, he or she will have something to say to you.

Socializers are the life of the party. They've got lots of things on their mind, they enjoy interaction, they thrive on connection with people, and they like a lively, direct pace. Talk show hosts Rosie O'Donnell, Oprah Winfrey, and Jay Leno all are classic socializer types.

Which of these styles describes you most accurately—the thinker, the relater, the director, or the socializer? You do have all four patterns in you, but one of those patterns is stronger and more dominant, and that's the pattern most people know you by.

The basic pattern, the dominant quadrant of your behavior, is your way of interacting with the rest of the world. And the reason there's a pattern to it is that we are designed to be creatures of habit. Habit's a good thing because it gives us a way to simplify our life. If we have to stop and think about how we're going to react to everything in great detail every single time, it wastes an awful lot of energy. So what we need is a comfortable pattern of doing things in a natural style that feels right to us.

Irritations

Let's look at each type in a little more detail. Imagine that we ask just a few basic questions.

- What sort of things would irritate thinkers? Thinkers are indirect and self-contained. Perhaps too much openness would be irritating. Being asked to "share something about yourself" in a group would cause alarm. Another irritant is disorganization. They are thorough and methodical and expect others to be the same.
- What would irritate relaters? Since relaters are easygoing and open, what irritates them is confrontation. They don't like getting into an awkward situation that might threaten their relationship with someone else. They like to avoid conflict. If things start getting awkward, relaters would rather withdraw or accommodate than risk upsetting the status quo. So if you want to stay on their good side, keep things smooth and pleasant as much as possible.
- What would irritate directors? Lack of results. Directors love to get things done, and anything that's going to slow them down is going to irritate them. I asked this of a seminar audience one time. I said, "Okay, directors, what is your greatest irritation?" One of the directors yelled out, "Slow drivers!" They also hate indecisiveness. They say, "Lead, follow, or get out of the way."
- What irritates socializers? Socializers are most irritated by being left out or ignored. They enjoy contact, connection, activity, being involved in things, and they want to be in the center of whatever's going on. And being left out makes them feel uncomfortable or as if they've done something wrong. To get along with socializers, bring them into the loop, keep them informed, send them update memos, leave messages.

Was one of these descriptions accurate in describing you? Which one? As we proceed, notice how many of the other descriptions seem to fit. The style that has the most consistency with your patterns is your natural style. You'll identify a little with each, but one will be the most natural fit.

Jobs

What kind of jobs would appeal to each of these styles?

- Thinkers might be drawn toward the exact sciences—accounting, science, medicine, computers, things like that—because they can use their high analytical skills. They can get into the details, and these jobs sometimes have less people interaction.
- Relaters might be drawn toward the professions of teaching, nursing, or counseling because they are based on one-to-one relationships.
- Directors might be called toward administrative positions: leadership, getting things done, being in charge, running things. This is because they want to see results, and when they are the leader they get to make sure the results will be achieved.
- Socializers might be drawn toward active fields like public relations, sales, or entertainment. All these professions have frequent people interaction tasks.

Of course you'll find all four behavioral styles in all different kinds of professions, but your natural inclination goes with your behavioral style.

Cars

What kinds of cars would a person of each different style drive?

- Directors might drive a big powerful car, dark color, huge engine, with the look of authority.
- Thinkers might drive something efficient, that had the kind of paint that wouldn't oxidize in sunlight, with all the dashboard gauges and dials that would tell them exactly how the machine is operating at any particular time, and it would have a warranty of 100,000 miles.
- Relaters might choose a car with lots of doors and lots of space to get people into it, like a van or a station wagon.

They'd buy a neutral color that was not offensive and didn't stand out too much, and they might ask for the horn to be disconnected.

- What might socializers choose? A red sports car, a motorcycle, a helicopter, something fun, something that would draw attention.

Anytime you understand someone else's behavioral style, you'll understand how you can best relate to him or her initially. This is like the tip of the iceberg of personality; it's the part you see most often. Under the surface, however, there's a lot more to personality: there are values, velocity, intellect. But on the surface we see the behavioral style, and if we can learn quickly to identify someone's style just by noticing the level of openness and the level of directness, then we can figure out how to get into alignment with him or her early in the relationship.

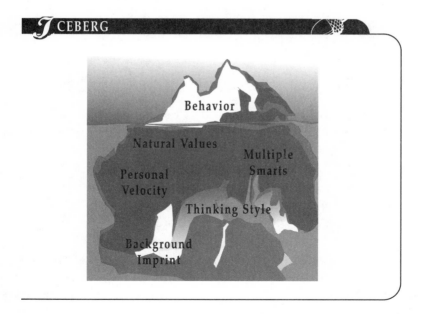

ICEBERG

Behavior

Natural Values

Multiple Smarts

Personal Velocity

Thinking Style

Background Imprint

Here's a quick summary of some of the characteristics of each of the styles.

The thinker. On the good side, thinkers tend to be orderly, precise, conscientious, neat, trustworthy, and careful. On the negative side of the equation, they tend to be a bit fearful, dependent, defensive, traditional, restrained, and nonexpressive.

The relater. On the good side, relaters tend to be loyal, attentive, patient, mellow, cooperative, pleasant. On the negative side, they tend to be indecisive, immobile, possessive, hesitant, and poor delegators.

The socializer. On the good side, socializers tend to be open and trusting, enthusiastic, compelling, optimistic, and charming. On the negative side, they tend to be overly emotional, gullible, superficial, highly talkative, imprecise, and unfocused.

The director. On the good side, directors tend to be leaders; they're good at initiating, and they're competitive, powerful, assertive, confident. On the negative side, they tend to be impulsive, forceful, pushy, inattentive, demanding, and impatient.

As I said before, you'll probably identify with traits from several of these styles. The key to this is to understand that all of us have a natural behavioral style that is our preferred way of dealing with the world. We can adapt and show a different style in a given situation, but that requires a lot of flexibility and versatility.

Now that you know your natural behavioral style, what do you do with this information? First, understand your nature and know your unique strengths and weaknesses. Next, recognize when your style enhances a situation or relationship and when it needs to be tempered or restrained. Also think about those three other styles that were not as strong for you and see if there is a secondary style in you that can be nurtured to expand your personality and flexibility.

Then reach out from your style and think of those who are close to you, in your family or in your immediate work group. What styles do they have? Recognize their unique strengths. Maybe you should be reaching out to them to help balance whatever limitations are inherent in your personal style.

BEHAVIOR CHART

	RELATER	THINKER	DIRECTOR	SOCIALIZER
Behavior pattern	Open/Indirect	Self-Contained/Indirect	Self-Contained/Direct	Open/Direct
Appearance	• Casual • Conforming	•Formal •Conservative	• Businesslike • Functional	• Fashionable • Stylish
Work space	• Personal • Relaxed • Friendly • Informal	• Structured • Organized • Functional • Formal	•Busy •Formal •Efficient •Structured	• Stimulating • Personal • Cluttered • Friendly
Pace	Slow/Easy	Slow/Systematic	Fast/Decisive	Fast/Spontaneous
Priority	Maintaining relationships	The task: the process	The task: the results	Relationship interacting
Fears	Confrontation	Embarrassment	Loss of control	Loss of prestige
Under tension will	Submit/Acquiesce	Withdraw/Avoid	Dictate/Assert	Attack/Be sarcastic
Seeks	Attention	Accuracy	Productivity	Recognition
Needs to know (benefits)	How it affects personal circumstances	• How logically to justify the purchase • How it works	• What it does • By when • What it costs	• How it enhances status • Who else uses it
Gains security by	Close relationships	Preparation	Control	Flexibility
Wants to maintain	Relationships	Credibility	Success	Status
Support his or her	Feelings	Thoughts	Goals	Ideas
Achieves acceptance by	•Conformity •Loyalty	•Correctness •Thoroughness	•Leadership •Competition	• Playfulness • Being entertained
Likes you to be	Pleasant	Precise	Practical	Stimulating
Wants to be	Liked	Correct	In charge	Admired
Irritated by	• Insensitivity • Impatience	• Surprises • Unpredictability	•Inefficency •Indecsions	•Inflexibility •Routine
Measures personal worth by	• Compatibility with others • Depth of relationships	• Precision • Accuracy • Activity	•Results • Track record • Measurable progress	• Acknowledgment •Recognition •Applause •Compliments
Decisions are	Considered	Deliberate	Definite	Spontaneous

The Four Styles in Action

Imagine white-water rafting down a river in the northern part of the United States. On the raft are four people: a relater, a socializer, a thinker, and a director. They're rowing along, and everything's going pretty smoothly, until all of a sudden there is a rumbling in the distance. This sound is coming from the next rapids—it's an enormous white-water rapid with rocks sticking up all over the place!

They look ahead in stark terror. The first one on the raft to speak is the director, who grabs an oar, leans directly toward the oncoming rapids, starts paddling, and then says, "All right, let's go!"

About that time, the relater says, "Wait a minute! We've all got to work together as a team!"

The socializer says, "Hold it! Hold it! Let me get my camera! I've got to capture this thing on film!"

And the thinker is turned a little bit away from the group, punching on a calculator. The director says, "What are you doing?"

The thinker says, "I'm trying to figure the odds of us coming out of this alive."

When the four types are not flexible, they can be the greatest possible irritation to one another. But when they are flexible, they can make a wonderful team. A director takes charge. The socializer sees to it that everybody's ideas get expressed in the most vivid way and everyone gets heard. The relater sees to it that all the personal needs are attended to and each person feels a part of the group. The thinker sees to it that all the details are handled and everything makes sense.

When people work together in concert, they're in alignment. Alignment produces harmony, and harmony produces great outcomes.

THOUGHT BREAK
- Which style do you exhibit most often?
- When does it work? When does it need to be tempered?
- What style is your spouse or partner? Is it different from yours?
- How do you decide things between you to make your relationship work?

10. Understanding Your Background Imprint: Nature + Nurture = Growth

The famous retailer J. C. Penney once said that none of us needs to live a minute longer as we are, because the Creator endowed us with the ability to change ourselves. My friend and fellow professional speaker Phillip Wexler says that the human being is the only creature on earth that is not the prisoner of its programming, but the master of it. There are parts of you that can change. And there are parts of you that can't change, nor would you gain anything by changing them.

You and I are the products of nature and nurture. *Nature* is who you are, your *entelechy*, the seed within you. That part will never change; it will merely unfold. *Nurture* is what you experience, how your growth is shaped by people and events. This part can change in many ways. In this chapter I'll focus on nurture, on how you can guide and groom and grow yourself in the ways that you want to grow.

Nature + Nurture = Growth. Whatever you lack in your essential nature can be augmented by acquiring the resources and support to fill the gaps. With that in mind, anything you want to achieve is probably within your grasp. Somebody somewhere has the answers you need and the resources you require for any goal you set.

My wonderful friend, the late Og Mandino, was the author of books, like *The Greatest Salesman in the World,* that have sold tens of millions of copies worldwide. In his speeches he often told the story of a boy who awoke one morning to find that a windstorm had blown a tree onto his bicycle. As he tried to free the bike from beneath the tree, his father asked why he hadn't pulled it free. He answered his father, "I'm using all my strength and it just won't budge." To this, his dad said, "No, son, you're not using all your strength. You haven't asked me to help."

Our strength doesn't lie within us only; it exists throughout the world and in other people with whom we can connect to do most anything we can dream of doing. Part of your strength lies in your background, the things you've known, seen, done, heard, and experienced. These are part of who you are. Part of your strength comes from the challenges you have accepted and overcome. Part of your strength comes from the coaching, support, encouragement, and strokes you received from others. And part of your strength still lies within others to whom you are connected and others to whom you aren't yet connected.

If you had access to lots of resources, if mentors were available to you, if your young life was filled with love, coaching, support, encouragement, and success in overcoming obstacles, then your background is considered enriched. That means you had a good foundation on which to build your self-esteem. You had a head start in most situations, and you experienced very little self-doubt compared to most other people.

But if the only time you heard "Well done!" was when your parents ordered steak, or if there was very little encouragement or praise, then your background would be comparatively unenriched or even disadvantaged. Even if you were fairly well supported, if you had few resources with which to advance, then you had more of a handicap than a head start. In this case, you'll need to "manage" your background.

That's right. You can manage your background. No, you can't go back in time and change what has already happened, but starting today you can have new experiences that tomorrow will have become part of your background.

If you consciously select the elements today to enrich your background tomorrow, then over a short time you'll have upgraded your own background. Too many people carry their background around with them as if it's a burden that is keeping them from living the rest of their life.

Your background is an extremely important part of who you are, but it isn't cast in concrete. You can get over it. Or, as a popular T-shirt states: It's never too late to have a happy childhood. Every day you have new experiences which, tomorrow, will be part of your background.

You can even break patterns that have gone on for generations. In the movie *Dragon: The Bruce Lee Story,* his mentor told him: "You have to conquer the demons inside you. Otherwise you will pass them on to your children." The demons are your fears; you have to face them and defeat your fears. All courage and strength must be developed by facing our fears and then transcending them.

If your background was disadvantaged, how was it disadvantaged? Did you get little encouragement or few breaks? Did you lack mentors or contacts? Were you the odd-person out—either you were brilliant and all your friends were ordinary or vice versa? What is an advantage in one context can be a terrible burden in another. Michael Jordan's height is great on a basketball court but a trial when he tries to fit into cars, airplane seats, or standard-size clothing. He also finds it tough to blend into a crowd.

While looking at the possible disadvantages of your background, also try to identify the corresponding advantages. One woman I know was adopted into an extremely abusive family. It was not a situation that any child should be reared in, yet she survived and came away with a determination to raise her own children with love and kindness. She also devotes most of her time to helping other families break the cycle of abuse. She is very effective because she's been there.

On the other hand, situations that look highly advantaged often carry their own seeds of disadvantage. Sometimes life comes too easily. Children who've been protected and had their paths smoothed may not be able to tolerate the ups and downs of later life. Most of us received advantages and disadvantages from our background. Review your early life and determine how it has affected your life. What were the advantages and disadvantages you were given: genetic pluses and minuses, emotional support and guidance, mentors, counselors, role models, learned attitudes, educational opportunities, connections and contacts, and exposure to different attitudes and cultures?

T H O U G H T   B R E A K

If you didn't have your background, you couldn't be who you currently are. What pluses have come from your negative experiences?

Another way to manage your background is to study it, to become more aware of the effects that it's had on you. Start by asking yourself, "Where'd I get that idea? Did it come from my parents, teachers, or friends influencing me?" Maybe the idea came from a book or directly from your own experience. Find out where.

Or ask yourself, "What causes me to feel like this? Did I see someone else respond this way? Did someone tell me this is how I should feel? Did I see this situation on TV?" We often learn about how to respond by watching others. Where have you seen this?

Many times, we just get into a habit. We always respond the same way, even though the situation might really be very different. We think we hear the same trigger words, and we're off, responding by reflex.

By linking stimulus and how you naturally respond, you'll discover some old programs, some old response habits, that may no longer be serving you very well. In that case, make some new assumptions, gather some new beliefs that are more in line with your current desired lifestyle.

Managing the Imprint Your Experiences Have Left on You

"Your Honor, this defendant never had a chance. With a background like hers, anyone would have become a criminal. She was merely acting out what her childhood experiences had taught her." Courtrooms frequently hear arguments like this, justifying someone's behavior by citing the negative influences of others upon him or her.

Yet we also see recurring examples of people who, despite a horrific childhood or years in a prison camp, go on to become caring parents, generous friends, and inspiring leaders. You are not the product of your background alone, but it does have an influence on you. As Anthony Robbins says, "Your past doesn't equal your future."

The happy news is that we can "manage" our background and even change it intentionally. No, we don't erase what is there. We simply add each new day's experience to all our previous experiences, thereby changing the overall nature of our imprints.

You will always remember the significant events in your life. But the way you remember them and feel about them can be changed based on how you choose to think about them.

> THOUGHT BREAK
>
> Make a list of the influences that shaped you. Note the people, events, experiences, feelings, and statements that were important to you. Take some time and give serious thought. Make the list as long as you like. Good and bad. Important and trivial. If it matters to you, it counts.
>
> Next, look over your list and rank the strength of influence each person or thing had on you. Note C for moderate impact, B for significant impact, and A for profound impact. Don't fret over your rankings, just separate the items as best you can for now.

Look over the list. Notice the A items. What would happen if you changed the *negative* As into Cs? You can, you know. As my friend W. Mitchell says, "It's not what happens to you that counts. It's how you react to it." He should know. Despite being horribly burned and greatly disfigured in one accident and wheelchair–bound by another, he is a cheerful, gracious, and inspiring professional speaker. With multiple justifications for being depressed, he is instead prosperous and surrounded by new friends he has made since his misfortunes.

Reframe your experiences. Take the worst items on your A, B, and C lists and convert them into Ds, things that have a minimal impact on you. Easy for me to say? Yes, but not that hard for you to do either. Just take your biggest burden and refile it in your mind under the category of "things that used to be a big deal but no longer are."

Perhaps this exercise seems silly to you, a bit meaningless and futile. After all, what's done is done, you can't change the past. Actually, you can change the past, or at least the way it influences you.

Sure, you'll still have your emotional triggers or hot buttons that set off an involuntary reaction in you. But you can learn to manage these events by refocusing your thoughts on what you want instead of what you fear or dislike. You are not destined to become your dad or mom. Nor are you programmed to turn out in a specific way. You choose your fate by selecting which parts of your nature to nurture.

If you tend to have a short temper, you could easily nurture it into a full-blown rage. Or you could diminish its impact by cultivating healthier thinking. I used to get really angry at bad drivers. It used a lot of my energy and often spoiled my entire day. Then I learned to rethink my reactions to them.

Rather than criticize their ancestry and honk my horn, I now ease up on the accelerator, give them the right-of-way, and say a quick prayer that they don't hurt anybody. Now, understand that I still think they are inconsiderate jerks. I just don't choose to let them make me angry. It took a few years to cultivate this skill, but it worked. I have fewer angry moments now because I changed the way I thought about or reacted to others' behavior. You can do the same with your background. Reframe the negatives and praise the positives.

Give yourself credit for your successes. Acknowledge how far you've come. Think of all the others who never got as far as you. Recall the obstacles you've overcome. Notice how much you now know. The simple fact that you are reading this book puts you miles ahead of most people in the world. Two billion people on this planet don't have access to electricity. Millions of them can't read. Millions more can't afford a book. And, tragically, of all those who can read and buy a book, millions don't choose to. They don't take time to enrich their minds and try to enhance the world. But you did. So give yourself some credit for being on the right path.

Your background is a storehouse of information from which to learn, not a burden you must drag through each day. Study your successes, learn from your failures. Let your past stay in the past. The future you see defines the person you'll be.

What stimulates us to respond a certain way? All of our responses evolve along the lines of our primary focus, our interests, our "meaning."

We are, as all of life is, self-organizing systems. That is, we organize around meaning. If a goal or interest has meaning to us, we alter our behaviors around it. We ignore what seems meaningless and attend to what we care about. This could be standing still to savor a sunset, running to catch a train, being quiet to relax and rest, or working tirelessly to build a career. It could be actively listening to your child or loved one, or speaking up in public to defend your rights. We attend meetings when we feel that value or enjoyment is to be gained there. We seek certain foods when we have a specific hunger or craving (How about Italian food tonight?). We cooperate with those who are aligned with us on some level and instinctively resist those who threaten us or what we care about.

Everything we do is stimulated by some basic human need. Everything we do comes down to a need that wants to be satisfied. The need is then transformed into a behavior by our beliefs and our assumptions. There are four basic human needs: (1) survival and safety, (2) love and belonging, (3) significance and self-respect, and (4) growth and becoming. The best-known research on this model was done by Dr. Abraham Maslow, a psychologist and author who studied psychology with an emphasis on the personality of the "self-actualized" person. His book *Motivation and Personality* is a classic. My model here is a simplified version of his concept.

Everything you do ultimately comes from one of those four levels of need. More specifically, our behavior stems from the lowest level of dissatisfaction. Think of it this way: Put each of those four levels on a ladder with survival at the bottom and growth at the top. As one need is met, we progress to the next level.

For instance, if you've just been told that you will be laid off from your job in two weeks, you might respond by focusing all your concerns on survival. That's natural. You'll worry about how to pay the rent or provide for the kid's education. Your need for safety might lead you to take the first offer of a job so all those things—the rent, the food, the education—will remain safe. Even if you know that the new job isn't right for you, you'll look to satisfy your need to survive first, before any other considerations. It's like missing a meal. At first you hardly notice it, but as time wears on you become aware of your hunger. And if you don't stop to eat, before long the only priority in your life is getting fed. Your first priority is to survive. However, once you're sure you'll survive and be safe, you can notice the need for belonging and love, the need to connect with other people. You move up a rung on the ladder.

When your need for love and belonging are not yet satisfied, all your behavior will be focused on ensuring that those needs get filled. When the need for love and belonging is met, you feel

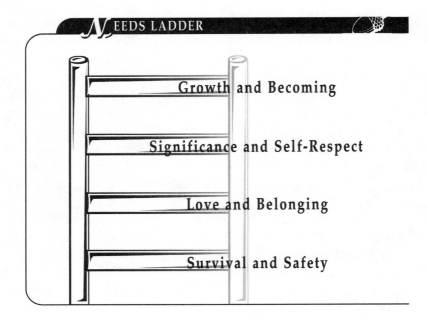

NEEDS LADDER

Growth and Becoming

Significance and Self-Respect

Love and Belonging

Survival and Safety

the need to make your mark in the world, to be significant. The view from the third rung sure is different from the prior two!

Significance and self-respect are esteem needs. Maslow splits esteem into two categories. One kind of esteem is the desire for achievement, for mastery and competence, for confidence to face the world, and for independence and freedom. The other side of esteem is the desire for reputation or prestige, status, fame, recognition, attention, dignity, or appreciation. When you satisfy the need for esteem, you feel self-confident, adequate, useful, and necessary in the world. At this level you may even be willing to risk safety or relationships to attain your goals. But not for long.

From there you see one more rung on the ladder and you become conscious of your inner potential. You seek ways to become more and to grow, to express what is in you.

In fact, Maslow says that you will become restless and discontented until you do what you were meant to do. In *Motivation and Personality* he writes, "A musician must make music, a builder must build, an artist must paint, a poet must write, if he is to be ultimately at peace with himself. What a man can be, he must be." How do you express who *you* really are?

Where are you on the ladder today? At different times in your life, you will be on different rungs. Situations can take us down a rung or two even while we strive to be on another. In an effort to achieve some goal in your career, you may all of a sudden be threatened by a fire or disaster and be yanked back to the safety and survival level in an instant. The situations change constantly.

The more you know about your placement on the ladder, the more accurate your assumptions and beliefs will be. To expand your awareness and ultimately guide your behavior, start asking yourself, "Where did I get that idea, and do I want to keep it? Is that idea serving me well?" Your beliefs don't have to control you; you can learn to control them. You can learn from your own experience by expanding your self-awareness and studying your background.

Another way to control your beliefs is first to control your behavior. Dale Carnegie said, "It's easier to act yourself into good thinking than it is to think yourself into good action." Just thinking about it won't make it happen.

In the book *Self Creation,* Dr. George Weinberg said, "Every time you act, you strengthen the thinking behind that act. To start controlling your behavior, every day find one way to act happier." I don't think he's suggesting that you hide your true feelings or lie and say, "Everything is wonderful!" when it's not, but I do find that when you start acting happy, you feel happier. Act as a successful person does and you'll *be* more successful. It's amazing how everything changes when you do.

In 1972 I was a clerk for the Little Rock Housing Authority in Arkansas. That's the Urban Renewal Agency. My salary was near minimum wage, I was married and had a small son at home, and my career seemed to be in "park." One day I heard the voice of Earl Nightingale on the radio. On that particular day, in his message, he said, "If you will spend one extra hour each day in study in your chosen field, you will be a national expert in five years or less." I thought, *Five years or less? I'm a government worker; I've got eight hours a day. I could do it by Thursday!* Then I started thinking, *Wait a minute! I'm working in a position that calls for very little initiative on my part.* I just filled out forms and did some filing; it was a very menial job. But in sitting there I had a lot of spare time to think about the things I wanted to think about. So I started studying different fields, trying to figure out what it was I wanted to do with my extra hour(s) each day. I finally discovered that what I liked the most was the field of personal development.

I set a goal to become an authority in the field of personal development. Now, you have to realize that at the time I set that goal, it was a ridiculously high goal. After all, I had no training or experience in that field.

Then I started studying everything I could get my hands on. In the evenings I'd listen to tapes, and during the day I'd read a book whenever I had a few spare minutes. I'd talk to people who seemed really to have their act together and see if I could learn from them. I'd go to seminars whenever I could. I joined the Jaycees and got involved in a program they called "Leadership in Action." All of this led me to be more and more sure that personal growth was the field I wanted to pursue.

Five years later to the day, sure enough, a magazine article I had written on the subject was published nationwide.

Beginning in 1977 I was training others full time, and I went on to achieve most of the goals I've ever set. It still amazes me that all these things were possible for me. Today, I'm constantly setting and reaching new goals. But wait just a second, let's go back to the reason I'm telling you this story. Why did I do it? Where was I on the needs ladder? Survival, love, significance, or growth?

I was surviving, so I was okay on the first rung of the ladder. I had a job, I felt loved, and had a good family relationship, so I was satisfied on the second rung of the ladder. And I seemed to have my esteem needs handled but not completely: I had never done anything that was really significant. I didn't feel like I stood out, like I had paid my dues and become *somebody* at that point in my life.

So that's what was motivating me, that was the need I wanted to fulfill—the need to feel significant. My belief was that I would like myself better, the world would like me better, and the world would be better off if I could help more people grow.

THOUGHT BREAK
- What level of the ladder have you been operating from lately?
- What could you do that would make you like yourself better?
- How could you help make the world a better place?
- If you were to spend an extra hour each day studying one subject, what would it be?

Build a New Background Imprint

Every day you choose actions and interactions that change your collective experience, your personal history. Each new relationship and experience becomes a part of tomorrow's background imprint. So as you progress through today, you are selecting your future *yesterdays.* For the Acorn Profile, answer this simple question: Is your current background imprint positive, neutral, or negative? Was it supportive, unsupportive, or somewhere in between?

Now use that awareness to make better choices each day.

11. Assembling Your Own Acorn Profile: An Overview of You

My velocity is high. Commitment, empathy, and knowledge are my top values. I'm a socializer type with a supportive background. I'm a conceptual thinker. Verbal and intrapersonal are my strongest intellects. Would you hire me as your accountant? How about as your child's baby-sitter? Perhaps as your personal assistant? Maybe as a speaker at your next convention?

When you know someone's profile, you know his or her natural strengths. People whose top values are knowledge, wealth, and commitment are well suited to accounting. The thinker style is suited to accounting work, as is mathematical intellect. Baby-sitters are probably more effective when their highest values are commitment and empathy with a strong interpersonal intellect and a relater style. Personal assistants do best with moderate velocity and fairly low power values. Relater or thinker styles tend to be the most accommodating. But there are always exceptions. **Your profile doesn't determine whether you can do well at something. It merely determines whether you will find it fulfilling.** You could probably do very well at several things that you wouldn't particularly enjoy. But why do that if you don't have to?

These are not rules. They are probabilities. But they are more reliable than general guesses or one-dimensional assessments like age, job experience, or education. What you know or have experienced doesn't necessarily tell you if you're right for a role. But your Acorn Profile certainly does.

The Acorn Profile is the composite of your traits as defined in the various chapters of this book. It is the overview of you as a person, or, as my wife, Paula, says, the "inner view."

You wouldn't expect to find the same profile in a waiter and a schoolteacher, or a sales representative and an accountant, or a military officer and a banker, or a retail clerk and a technician. Different profiles fit different situations. Now, the world is not so perfectly balanced that we can all just go only where there's a natural fit, but having this knowledge of profiles certainly allows you to make better choices for yourself.

There are aspects of all jobs, all situations, and all relationships that aren't aligned with our nature, but by knowing where the differences are we can lessen the negative effect. We can do what I call job tailoring or situation tailoring: just take it in a little bit here, let it out a little bit there, make it a more perfect fit.

By the way, the same thing applies within your own personality. There are parts of you that probably seem to contradict other parts of you. Think about that for a second. What if you've got a director style, which is a no-nonsense, bottom–line–oriented, get–it–done style, together with low velocity? Hmm, that means that *your* get–it–done style prefers a smaller challenge. What if you're a high–velocity type with a relater style? Then you'll tend to be a person who takes on big challenges but in an easygoing, more interpersonal kind of way, like former U.S. President Jimmy Carter. What about a high wealth value together with poor spending habits?

Imagine going to meet someone for a business deal. You know nothing about the person except her company and title. You enter the meeting, and the person hands you a card that says "Acorn Profile." As you read it you note that it contains all the key categories that define the seed inside the person: how the person learns best, the net impact her background has had, her thinking style, top intelligences, strongest values, optimum velocity, and behavioral style. Imagine if you could get a card like that from every person you dealt with. What impact would that much self-disclosure have on your business discussion?

Obviously, it would have a huge impact. You would know how to present your information to get it understood, you'd know what pace to work at, you'd know which parts of your proposal would have the most or the least appeal. You'd have a sense of what behavior to expect from this person. You'd even have a pretty good idea of how self-assured the person was.

Could you do something useful with that much of an inside view? Sure you could. You'd know what a person was going to be like to deal with, you'd know how to put your information together to deal with her, you'd know a lot of things that most people don't know.

When's the last time you knew that much about someone else? Most of us don't even know that much about our spouse! Before we explore this further, notice what the profile does *not* tell you. It doesn't disclose age, sex, culture, race, religion, political party, education, club memberships, favorite teams, or even physical appearance, all of which some people use to discriminate against others.

Which elements of one's diversity are more meaningful?

External Diversity	Internal Diversity
Religion, beliefs	Natural values
Age, gender, health	Personal velocity
Education, credentials	Multiple intellects
SAT score, IQ rating	Thinking style
Language, lifestyle, social status	Behavorial style
Culture, race, job experiences	Background imprint
Political party, philosophy	Psychological blind spots

When you understand *internal* diversity, the rest of people's differences become less important. If we were able to know ourselves and each other that fully, most prejudice would be useless, and a lot of it would automatically stop. *The better we understand each other, the less we judge each other. The less we judge, the more we accept. The more we accept, the less we fear. The less we fear, the more we cooperate. The more we cooperate, the more we accomplish. And the more we accomplish, the better life is for all.*

Some Sample Cases

Joey and Jane had been married for twenty years. They had two children and a successful lifestyle. He was a schoolteacher and she had a small retail shop. Both were well educated and reasonably healthy. They had a wide circle of friends and their future looked bright . . . from the outside.

On the inside, things weren't so good. They bickered often. Their children were highly emotional, and they didn't have many truly happy moments together as a family. Sure, they had had fun in the past and accumulated lots of good memories. And yes, they were good parents in all the noticeable ways. The trouble was that they weren't a very good match for each other and neither of them realized it. Nor did either of them know what to do about it. So it affected both them and their children.

Both Joey and Jane were strategic thinkers. Both had socializer behavioral styles. Both were word smart. But that is where their similarities stopped. Joey was a high-velocity guy with a disadvantaged yet supportive background that, happily, motivated him to try even harder to succeed. Jane had only moderate velocity and an unsupportive background, which caused her constant self-doubt. She needed lots of reassurance and nurturing. He needed freedom to work and experiment. Though he tried to accommodate her, it was never enough. She didn't understand why he worked so much, and she took it as a rejection of her.

They both had high empathy and knowledge values, but his

highest value was wealth while her highest was power. Whereas he needed to achieve and build wealth, she needed to gain recognition and thrived on being in charge of things. Her constant need for attention distracted him from his projects. His constant need for achievement threatened her desire to feel significant. The irony is that they did in fact love each other. They just didn't know how to live together in harmony.

If they had been aware of each other's internal diversity, if each had known what the other truly needed in order to live fully and happily, they could have found many useful compromises. She would have realized that his high velocity had nothing to do with his feelings about her. He would have seen that her high power value called for a frequent sharing of the spotlight in their relationship. They could have cultivated their similarities in knowledge and empathy values and enjoyed each other's thinking style and socializer nature. Their relationship could have survived.

Dan is a high-powered business executive. He started in sales at a department store and quickly rose to the top. Then he left for a position in financial services consulting and rose even more quickly. Before long he had built a thriving multistate business with dozens of employees. But something was missing—he was still single.

When Dan started "shopping" for a soul mate he really took the task seriously. He did a lengthy self-analysis and took half a dozen psychological assessments to discover his nature. From all these tests he assembled the equivalent of an Acorn Profile. Then every time he started getting serious about someone he was dating, he would show her his Acorn Profile and help her build one of her own. Then they would discuss their differences and similarities.

This was not done in a clinical, impersonal way. It was a lively discussion of past experiences, future goals, previous dealings with people and situations, and personal likes and dislikes. As they truly got to know each other, it became obvious to both of them whether they were a good fit. When Dan finally got married, he chose a woman who was an almost perfect complement to his nature. She was a doctor with high velocity and a career of her own. Both of them had commitment, empathy, and knowledge as their top values. Their behavior styles were director and socializer. Each had a supportive background and strategic thinking bandwidth. Their top smarts were math and logic, followed by self and people smarts. They run marathons, are active in their community and in their respective professions, and live a very happy life.

Denise married Paul because she thought nobody else would ever ask her. It could have turned into a good marriage, but their lack of self-awareness aggravated their differences. He came from an impoverished background with very low self-esteem. She had a very supportive background yet also had a low regard for herself. Her velocity was moderate, his was low. She was a strategic thinker, he was operational. His top values were sensuality, power, and commitment. Hers were commitment, empathy, and aesthetics. Noticing a pattern here? They had very little in common. They endured for several years before finally divorcing. It was an intensely unpleasant divorce, and each of them blamed the other for the failure. The fact was, without a high level of self-understanding, they hardly had a chance. This was not an easy match even for the most self-aware people in the world.

When people are self-aware, they are more likely to find and cultivate their areas of compatibility. When they are not self-aware, their differences are more likely to be magnified. Seldom do people marry or form business partnerships with people who are perfectly compatible with them. Life isn't that generous to us. So we must learn to identify, understand, and connect with the internal diversity we encounter day to day.

Susan and Dana were excited about working together. Every time they met, their business discussions soared to new heights of quality and accomplishment. They seemed to feed each other's strengths, and besides, it was just plain fun to work together. So they formed a partnership. Details were worked out and plans made. All their assets were merged, and the new business was off and running. For almost four years they exceeded either of their previous track records. They also exceeded their goals.

Susan had a conceptual bandwidth, commitment, empathy, and knowledge as top values, a thinker behavior style, and was picture and word smart. Her velocity was high. So was Dana's. Dana had a strategic bandwidth, wealth, knowledge, and power values on top, a socializer style, and was math and people smart. Their smarts made a great and varied combination. They loved each other's thinking. Susan generated the most new ideas and Dana turned them quickly into dozens of strategies and plans. Their high velocities kept both of them going at a steady pace.

But Dana's wealth and power values were quite different from Susan's commitment and empathy values. At first, this was enjoyable, but after they had reached their common goals, their wishes were quite different. Through much discussion it became obvious that they did not have the same desires for their futures. So they split up.

Lest you misinterpret this situation, note that they split up amicably. They were not angry at each other. They did not resent each other. They simply realized that they had gone as far as it made sense to go together. Their shared goals had been achieved, and now their unique personal goals were pulling them in different directions. Because they were aware of their internal diversity, they could make good decisions without turning them into emotional issues.

Today Susan and Dana are still best friends and frequently collaborate on business dealings. Each is successful in her own right, and they enjoy each other thoroughly. They also understand each other thoroughly.

Andy and Kim are truly in love. Even after thirty years of marriage, they flirt and cuddle like newlyweds. He's a banker and she is a homemaker. When they got married, neither of them could speak "acorn." What I mean is, they didn't know themselves or each other very well. They just happened to find a good match. Not a perfect one, but a good one nonetheless.

Andy has high velocity, socializer style, word, self, and people smarts, and a strategic bandwidth. His background was supportive and he likes himself. He loves to learn (knowledge value) and enjoys helping others (empathy).

Kim is music smart and people smart, has low velocity and operational bandwidth. Her top values are empathy, sensuality, and commitment. Her background was supportive, and she has high self-esteem. A natural relater, she loves people and eagerly takes a supporting role in any situation.

In their early years, Andy and Kim had some rough times. They didn't stop loving each other, but they experienced many fears and doubts. She wanted him to be less ambitious (velocity differences) and more considerate of other people's needs (socializer style versus relater style). This caused him to feel hurt, since his high empathy value already caused him to care about the needs of others. He just didn't express it in the same ways as Kim. He also wanted her to stand up for herself more (again a style difference, directness) and to dream bigger dreams. High-velocity people set big goals; people with low velocity don't.

As they grew, Andy and Kim both became more self-aware. They attended seminars, listened to tapes, and read and discussed books on personality and psychology. This caused them not only to recognize their differences but also to embrace and celebrate them. Today, after thirty years, they talk openly about their traits and accept them as matter-of-factly as they would a difference in height.

> People who know themselves are easy to be around. They don't worry much about others judging them. They are comfortable with themselves and accept their shortcomings without complaint. If they were offered a high-paying job for which they were not qualified or suited, they wouldn't complain. Instead of getting depressed over not being up to the opportunity they were offered, they would merely say, "No, that's not for me," and happily go on with living.

Carol Jean was not suited for the job she wanted, but she was suited for the one she had. Not being very self-aware cost her a good job and spoiled a friendship. CJ's velocity was moderate, her bandwidth operational, background supportive, and behavior style relater. Her intellect was strongest in people and math. Her top values were wealth, commitment, and power.

CJ's job was telephone sales and account management. With a moderate velocity she worked steadily and well. Her confidence came from a good education and a supportive childhood. She made sales calls well. She was also good with numbers and kept detailed accounts of each of her clients and her own performance as well. She had a benevolent employer who shared information freely and frequently praised her for her work.

But she wanted to be the vice president of sales. Her wealth and power values were both addressed well through the position she had, but she felt she deserved to be running the entire sales department. She had let motivation go to her head without increasing her self-awareness. When questioned as to why she deserved it, she replied, "Because I have been here seven years and

Harriet [a woman with fewer years of experience who worked in another department] is getting paid more than me." What she was ignoring was that Harriet was better suited and more highly educated for her position, and her department was generating much more money than CJ's. One day CJ marched into her boss's office and demanded to be interviewed for the vice presidential position. She got her interview but spoiled her working relationship with the boss because of how she approached it. When she was not offered the position, she quit. What a shame.

Had CJ been aware that a vice presidential position was more suited to strategic thinking than operational, and that high velocity was more compatible with the workload there, she might have changed her goal. She was using the wrong stimulus for her growth. Jealousy is not an effective motivator. Competition, yes, but not jealousy. If CJ had gotten the position she wanted, she likely would have found the demands of the job daunting and would have been not only unhappy but also ineffective on the job. Had she stayed in her existing position and set achievement goals and earnings goals, she could have continued to increase her income, gotten the recognition she desired, and continued a happy career.

Profiling Groups

Here is a way the Acorn Profile can help you deal with groups. I once did a seminar for a group of Hollywood talent agents. In preparation for the program I got a profile of every person in attendance, almost a hundred people. Entering a roomful of strangers armed with their Acorn Profiles definitely increases your self-confidence as a speaker. I had spent an entire day studying their profiles and noticing how similar or dissimilar they were. I knew them well even though we'd never met.

It's fascinating that you can profile a group just as you can profile an individual. Remember, these were Hollywood talent agents. Here's their group profile; see if it fits your impression of what they would be like. They were strategic thinkers whose top intellects were verbal, interpersonal, and logical. High velocity, with neutral backgrounds, their top values were knowledge, power, and wealth. They also had a socializer behavioral style. Does that fit your image of a Hollywood talent agent?

That may seem like more information than you can process all at once, but let me walk you through it step by step. These agents were strategic thinkers, people whose job is to find bookings for the people they represent. As such, they constantly need to be looking for options and possibilities, thinking of new combinations of things to get a new outcome produced.

Their top intellects were verbal, interpersonal, and logical. What a perfect fit for them! A verbal intellect means they're good at finding ways to express things and get their message across to people. An interpersonal intellect means they understand thoughts and feelings. A logical intellect means they can put things together in a proposal that makes good sense.

These agents were also high velocity. It's a high-energy business with lots of requirements for late nights and early mornings, meetings with hundreds of people, all kinds of different phone calls to return at the last minute, lots of responsibility. Neutral backgrounds was another part of their profile. This was a group of a hundred people who'd come from a diverse mix of backgrounds, some of which were very supportive, while others were not supportive at all, but the net effect of it all was that background was generally neutral for them.

Their top values were knowledge, power, and wealth. These are people who want to know everything they can know in relation to their field. They love being in the spotlight, being in charge, and being noticed, and they are really money motivated. Finally, they fit the socializer style: businesspeople but party animals. Does that fit the image? I think so.

On another occasion, my good friend Captain Charles Plumb, a Navy officer and professional speaker, had invited me to speak to the officers and top enlisted personnel of his assigned unit. It was a very high-level unit with global responsibilities. The group included everyone from former top gun pilots to war heroes. Again, I had profiled all of them in advance. To introduce me, Charlie stood before the group in uniform and asked, "What do you know about me just from looking at me?" They responded by "reading" his uniform to him, as the insignias and ribbons had special meanings to them. They knew, for example, that he was a captain, a pilot, had served in Vietnam, had been a prisoner of war, and so forth.

Then Charlie took off his shirt and stood there in his T-shirt, asking the same question. "What do you know about me just by looking?" They started making jokes: It looks like you don't eat much, it looks like you probably work out pretty regularly . . . and other wisecracks. Charlie stopped them and asked, "Would it be helpful if I had some labels on my T-shirt that showed you what my intellect is, what my values are, my personal velocity, my behavioral style, and so forth?" They said that would be great. He said, "Well, I'm not the guy who can explain that to you, but our speaker this morning, Jim Cathcart, is. I think he can do the job just fine."

What a wonderful introduction! I gave them an overview of the Acorn Principle concept and explained the implications of their own Acorn Profiles. Incidentally, on the inside these people looked just like John Wayne. They had an operational get-it-done thinking style with logical, verbal, and physical smarts and moderate velocity. Their top values were commitment, knowledge, and sensuality, and their behavioral style was director. Though there were some exceptions, that was the overall nature of the group.

Why was all of this important? When I conducted that training I was able to identify directly with who they were, what they cared about, and how they thought, just as I had done with the Hollywood agents.

You can do the same thing. The more you start picking up elements of someone's Acorn Profile—either in casual conversation or through deliberate concentration—the more you will be able to adjust everything you do to be in perfect alignment with him or her, which gets you a much quicker and better outcome.

MY ACORN PROFILE

Natural Values (circle your three strongest)

Sensuality   Empathy   Wealth   Power

Aesthetics   Commitment   Knowledge

Personal Velocity (circle one)

High   Moderate   Low

Thinking Style (circle one)

Conceptual   Strategic   Operational

Background Imprint (circle one)

Highly supportive   Somewhat supportive   Not supportive
and positive   and positive   or positive

Multiple Intellects (circle your three strongest)

Verbal   Interpersonal   Mathematical   Visual

Musical   Physical   Intrapersonal

Behavior Style (circle your dominant style)

Relater   Socializer   Thinker   Director

Sources of Truth (circle the three you trust the most)

Scientific analysis   Intuition   Authorities

Feelings   Personal experience   Reasoning

What does your Acorn Profile help me know and understand about you? What insight does that profile give me? Ooh, lots of things. It helps me understand why some things come easily to you and other things are hard. It helps me understand why you just click with some people, and other people you find it awkward to relate to at all. It helps me to understand that by your nature you move toward or away from certain situations. It helps me figure out why you care so much about certain aspects of a situation and not much at all about other aspects of it. The better we understand the patterns in us, the better we can make choices that cause our life to be in alignment with our nature instead of opposed to it.

To define your own Acorn Profile, we will look at what comprises your seed. That is what this section is about. It is your guided tour of yourself.

Your Acorn Profile

Look over your profile and try to forget who it is. Be totally objective, as if you were looking at the profile of a stranger. Just look at the elements and the patterns. Using only the information in front of you, describe this person. For example, I might look at mine and say, this person is someone with high energy who likes to take on big goals and enormous challenges, so I'm describing high velocity. This person believes very strongly in doing the right thing (which would be high commitment value), loves to learn (high knowledge value), and genuinely feels a need to be connected to other people (high empathy value). This person's thinking style leads him to think first about concepts and the big picture, then about all the possibilities and later about the applications. So that's conceptual thinking followed by strategic and then operational. I could go through anyone's profile and describe him or her to you in detail, and you'd start knowing how to deal more effectively with that person.

Take a moment now to stop and record your description of this person with your profile. Just write a little narrative, a paragraph or two describing you—not the you that you know, but the you that appears in that profile—and keep that together with your profile. Pause now and do that exercise.

Once you've completed that exercise, let me ask you some

questions about it. How much were you able to notice just from the profile? How close was the description that you wrote to who you know yourself to be? Chances are that about 85 percent of your profile was right on. It is much easier to be objective about others, but even our own profile can help us make some useful observations about ourselves.

How can people easily gather this kind of information about each other? Well, first they've got to get accustomed to noticing more. Second, start looking for ways to share elements of your own profile, a little more self-disclosure with people you trust. Third, keep a record of this information together with your notes on this. When you restudy this or rethink yourself, review your notes and reflect on how well you've gotten to know people on the inside. For job interviews, have a person study this material and complete a questionnaire for you. Or give him or her a questionnaire to gather the kinds of information you've learned from this.

Another idea is to make a game of this, either alone or with friends who've read this material. Select a person known by all of you (such as a famous figure or someone in your family or community) and profile him or her. Write the profile on only one major part of the person, like velocity or values, then describe the profile aloud and see how well it fits the person you know. You may even agree to profile each other. Do the profile without the person being present, discuss it briefly with some other people, then call the person in and get his or her reaction. After a business meeting with someone, make a habit of writing some quick notes about his or her profile and keep that with your other business notes related to that person. This way you can review it prior to the next meeting.

Remember, you could be wrong while doing this, but you're still doing more and noticing more than 99 percent of other people are. So even with some errors, you're still going to be miles ahead. Besides, the alternative is to notice less. There is so much more to people than this profile. You are not your profile.

But your profile sure gives a good insight into who you are. Think about all the diversity within people: birth order, life cycles and passages that we go through, learned values we pick up from various sources, and neurolinguistics, meaning whether we process information more through our feelings, hearing, or vision.

There's also left-brain and right-brain dominance, whether your cerebral or your limbic brain tends to play the stronger role in who you are, different philosophies, different cultures, religions, holistic systems, genetic encoding, traditional psychology, and so on. There's so much to know about people!

The Acorn Profile is simply a starting point to help you explore all the endless aspects of being human. Notice more in all ways you can.

My final question about *your* Acorn Profile is whether this is the profile of the person you *want* to be. Have you grown the way you like? Do you see areas you would like to change? Are you out of alignment in some areas? Where do you need to reconnect with your nature?

THOUGHT BREAK

To start reconnecting with your natural possibilities, ask yourself, "How could I be more me? Where would I live? How would I structure my typical day? What would I do for a living? Who would my friends be? What books would I read? What foods would I eat? What would people say about me?"

Only you can create your future. Is it time now to make some realignments? How could you tailor your life to be a little better fit for you? What do you like most about yourself? What would you like to change?

Can you see more of the acorn in others? How can that help your relationship with them?

Section Three

Nurture Your Nature

"Mr. Sam, I'd like you to meet Jim Cathcart. He's doing a seminar today for our management team." That's how I was introduced to the patriarch of WalMart, Sam Walton. I was in Bentonville, Arkansas, at their headquarters to train them in "Helping People Grow."

"Mr. Sam" was gracious and friendly. He took the time to make me feel welcome. This man has had arguably the largest impact on the retail merchandise business of anyone who ever lived. His ideas and the talents of hundreds of thousands who connected with him have revolutionized the way products get to market these days.

Yet Sam himself was a simple man without an advanced education. He did not assert a power image and manipulate things for his own gain. He took a fanatical dedication to serving people and created an empire that could make it happen.

Your success, like Sam Walton's, will depend not on your education or negotiating skills. It will grow out of using the potential that lives within you. You will succeed by nurturing the seed, your seed.

Now that you've discovered many parts of that seed, let's put it to work. This section will show you how to activate the growth hormones in you. Your Acorn Profile can be your guide to tapping your potential. As you rethink your goals and aspirations, review your profile with an eye toward finding your *natural* path. When you grow your inner circle of relationships, do so with an awareness of each person's Acorn Profile.

Look for alignment with people and make choices that allow you to be more of your natural self. If you merely align your life 10 percent more each year, in a few years you will have a near-perfect fit between who you are and what you do day to day. Life may not be perfect, but you can *perfect* it through better choices of how you live it.

An abundant life awaits you.

12. How Your Relationships Define You: Growing Your Inner Circle

If you don't understand your relationships, you don't fully understand yourself. Your relationships are the essence of your life experience. They are not separate from you; they are part of you. Your relationships define you.

Is the idea that your relationships define you surprising? You might ask, "What about my acorn, my individuality, my *self*— aren't *those* what define me?" Think about it this way: Life exists only in the interactions between entities. Richard Lewontin, a geneticist, was recently quoted by author Meg Wheatley as having said, "The environment is an organized set of relationships between individuals." In other words, your interactions are your life; you define yourself through your relationships. The people you choose to spend time with show what you think of yourself and your place in the world. A quick way to know more about you is by meeting the people you spend your time with.

As humans, it's our nature to be social beings. By that I mean we choose to live together in a community, in a society, for the common good of all of us. And we mold our own communities by the people we decide to connect to.

Who's in *your* community? Your closest social contacts in your community might be with your immediate family, your spouse, your father and mother, and your siblings. Your extended community can also be other relatives, or perhaps your neighbors, or your associations and affiliations such as your church or clubs. And with each person in our community we have some sort of a relationship, some sort of connection, and some unique way we act out that relatedness. For instance, you might keep in contact with your family by a phone call once a week or once a month. Or maybe you have a good friend you have lunch with regularly. Or maybe you just see people at a club, church, or a meeting, and you always stop and talk for a few minutes. All of these are relationships, each at a different level, each with a different impact on you.

In this chapter I'd like to guide you through a deeper understanding of the nature of your relationships. Why look at relationships? Aren't they outside your nature? No, they're not, because we express and understand ourselves through our relationships. How you relate to others and how they relate to you, how those relationships nurture you, whether those relationships have quality and purposefulness, can very much nurture your nature. In fact, once established, your relationships become a part of your nature and you become a part of theirs. As you grow, you become a vital part of your network, your ecosystem. Others depend on you and you depend on them. You no longer exist as separate and alone.

My most active relationships are with my wife, son, mother, office staff, best friend (a colleague), partners in two other businesses, the proprietors at my favorite local restaurants, my travel agent, literary agent, and colleagues with whom I serve on committees, boards, and projects. There are many more people in my life, but these are the ones I interact with most often.

Let's look at the people closest to you. Pull out your daily calendar and look over the last several months to see whom you've had the most contact with. Next, look through your phone numbers and see whom you call the most. Then skim your Christmas card list or your address book and notice whom you come in contact with the most. Make a separate list of the people with whom you interact most often.

The records may surprise you. You may not realize who constitutes your circle of *frequent* contacts. People often go for months on end without contacting some of the people they care most about and feel closest to. Sometimes we think we've been very much in touch with people with whom we've been out of touch. And I can guarantee you that if there's been no contact, the relationship has not grown stronger. Contrary to popular myth, absence does not make the heart grow fonder; it simply blurs the memory. Out of sight can mean out of mind.

Were there any surprises for you in this exercise? Did you think you had more contact than the data showed? Now that you've looked it over, do you really have a relationship or just an acquaintance? Sure, we all have special relationships that can instantaneously pick up where we last left off, but not with everyone. Most relationships need to be nurtured, watered like a plant, to grow.

So let's stay focused on the people you are most in contact with these days, especially those you value the most, the ones I call your inner circle. If you picture the circle of people most important in your life and your career right now, who's in that circle?

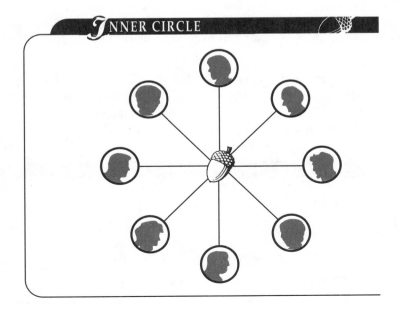

INNER CIRCLE

Count the number in your inner circle and try to limit your inner circle to twelve or fewer for this illustration. Take a piece of paper and write their names in circles around you in the center like lollipops attached to the hub of a wheel, each circle represents a person, and the stick that connects you to them represents your relationship with that person.

In the area outside that, write the names of people in your outer circle if you want. These names would be those people you don't make contact with that often but who are important to you anyway.

Don't bother with lines or circles for the outer circle; just write the names out there in the margins so that you can look back later and keep them loosely in mind. Now, when you do this exercise, what you'll have is a page with lots of names on it.

Some people come up with only five in their inner circle. Others have a full twelve, and sometimes people choose to create one with more than twelve, but that makes the model a little harder to work with. Try to identify only your inner few. Don't list the ones you *wish* were there; list only the actual, key players in your life for right now. Later you can make changes.

What purposes do other people serve in your life? Look over both your inner and outer circles. Notice all the inner circle people and ask yourself, "Of all the people here, whom can I most confide in? Whom can I brag to? Whom can I be silly with? Who are my playmates? Whom can I compete with happily? Who inspires me? Who brings out my potential? Who encourages me by his or her example to be a better person?"

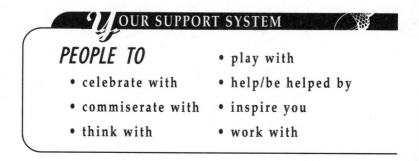

YOUR SUPPORT SYSTEM

PEOPLE TO

- celebrate with
- commiserate with
- think with
- play with
- help/be helped by
- inspire you
- work with

Ask, "Who are my mentors? Whom can I turn to or be nurtured by without him or her trying to fix me? With whom can I explore ideas? With whom can I just be myself? Who can I cry in front of? Who will collaborate and plan with me? Who believes in me? Whom do I just really like to be around? Whom do I love, and who loves me?"

These are pretty significant questions, because we're talking about the essence of being alive. All of those actions and interactions are the reasons we need other people in our lives.

And I'll bet as you looked over that list of questions, a lot of those roles didn't have names to go with them. Rarely does one person have people to play all of those life roles. But just knowing what's missing puts you ahead of the game, because now you can cultivate those qualities in the existing relationships and/or look for new friends to fill the empty roles. Be careful not to fall into the trap of expecting one person to be all those things for you. It isn't possible, nor would it be fair to expect it.

Three Essentials for a Healthy Relationship

Now let's look at the circles around the hub, your inner circle. (Please write out your inner circle now so that you apply this information to actual people who are currently active in your life.) In each of those relationships I'd like you to assess where you stand on the three essentials for a healthy relationship. Look at the people on your list and consider each one of them. These essentials for a healthy relationship are based on the work of Drs. David and Vera Mace, founders of the Association of Couples for Marriage Enrichment. What they found about couples applies every bit to other relationships as well.

1. **The first essential is mutual commitment to make the relationship work.** Both of you have to be working to make this one turn out well. If only one of you is committed to making the relationship work, you can bet that it has a limited future.

2. **The second essential is open, frequent communication.** You've got to stay in touch, and the quality of the contact has to be honest; it must be okay to tell each other the truth.

3. **The third essential is clear agreements.** The better we understand what we expect from each other, and the more clearly we have agreed on what we're going to do with each other, the better we are able to resolve conflict and overcome obstacles.

Assess Each Relationship

For each of your relationships, make a note on the line that represents your relationship which of those three essentials you have and which you need. The ones you need are your homework. As you do this all around the wheel, you will be evaluating not only your team but also your relationship with each member of it. And you will see what's missing and what's strong in each relationship.

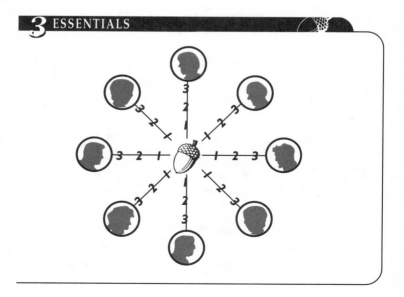

With one person, you may need to talk about how committed you are to making this relationship turn out well. With another, you may just need to open up the communication. With still another, you may need to clarify your agreements and expectations of each other. By working on the three essentials, you'll be doing the best work you can toward growing the potential within your circle.

If you notice a pattern in the numbers, for example, all of them are missing a 1, it tells you something about yourself. You may be reluctant to commit to relationships; therefore, that's what you get in return from others.

If there are lots of 2s missing, perhaps you should work on your own openness with others. Practice disclosing more about yourself or your feelings. Tell the whole truth more often. You may be holding back, thinking that the less you share of data, information, or personal feeling, the safer you'll be. Not true. The less you commit to your connections with others, the less you'll get from those relationships. Withholding information makes relationships mere transactions, and neither party is benefited.

If number 3 is the most rare in your assessment, work on clarifying your expectations with others. Get into the habit of bringing up your expectations. Say, "As I understand it, you'd like to see X happen. Is that accurate?" Then describe your expectations. Clarify what both of you may be assuming is so. The clearer your agreements are, the more likely you are to fulfill them.

Assess Each Individual

Do an Acorn Profile of all people in your circle. Notice how they think, what they value, what their velocity is, how their background influences them, their behavioral style, and more. Write it down. Keeping this kind of record to help you study your key relationships will help you achieve more alignment with each of them. Update and refine the profiles over time.

Notice their similarity and differences from your profile. Notice the patterns of profiles within the group.

Assess the Overall Group

Now forget momentarily that this is your personal circle; just look at the people in it. Based on what you know about these people, what kind of a resource team would they make? Look at them from the perspective of a group of people who are a resource to you. I know that most likely these people do not interact directly with one another. They are mostly "community" only in the sense that they interact with you as the common denominator. But if you had to go to these people to be a resource for you for anything you might need, how would they measure up? Would you consider them highly capable, well educated, versatile, focused, mature, sophisticated, financially smart, fun?

The better you know the group, the more accurately you can predict their capabilities. Stop for a moment. This is *your* inner circle we're talking about. These are the people through whom you live a great deal of your life. So take a moment to remind yourself of the goals and dreams you have for yourself over the next several years. Just picture your near future as you would *like* it to be.

Now ask yourself, "How well does my current inner circle support my plans to achieve those goals? Are they the team that can take me there, or do I need some new players?" If you don't have the talents, skills, and traits on your team that you need to reach your goals, then it's time to go shopping. This doesn't mean you have to dump any good friends, just add some new ones. It's time to find new resources.

Grow a Greater Resource Network

What resources will you need to achieve your goals? Here are some resources to consider. How about financial savvy? Many times our family or close friends may not be the best sources of financial expertise.

To achieve your goals, you may need people around you who have clear thinking and good connections. Does your inner circle provide the encouragement and support you need?

What kind of skills do they have as good planners, persuasive sales types, visionary thinkers, good problem solvers, team builders, pragmatic get-it-done types?

Maybe you need others who fill in the skills you lack. Perhaps someone who inspires you to grow and achieve more. Maybe the resources you need are artists or playful types who bring out your creativity and humor. Do you sometimes just need a sympathetic listener, someone who can listen without offering solutions or judgments, someone who won't tolerate excuses and forces you to face facts?

Maybe you live only by the rules and you need someone around you to remind you that sometimes the things you think are rules are merely guidelines, and you can think outside the box.

And maybe the hardest of all is to seek a devil's advocate, someone who will challenge your ideas, who will oppose your good ideas so that they can become even better. Do you need this type of person?

What skills and qualities do you need on your team to achieve your goals? Note your needs now.

When you find the skills, attitudes, and support you need among your inner circle, let those people know they play a role in helping you achieve your goals. Let them know you appreciate their contribution. And let them know how valued they are.

If you find that you're lacking the resources you need from your inner circle to help you achieve your goals, then keep your eyes and ears open for new friends and associates to round out your team. Go shopping for new people. If your team doesn't contain the qualities you need, your goals will be harder to achieve. And likewise it will be harder to become the person you want to become if you're not in touch with others of similar character. Lift your sights, hold yourself to higher standards, and bring out the best that is in you.

Your Inner Circle

This brings me to the topic of you nurturing your inner circle relationships. Besides what you get from them and how they help you achieve your goals, how can you improve these relationships and have richer inner circle relationships?

As I stated earlier, a society or community is a group of people who choose to live together for the good of all of them. So this is not a one-way street. Besides them helping you achieve your goals, you can help them. Here are some suggestions for richer inner circle relationships that are beneficial to both of you.

For many of your friends, the best starting point would be simply to spend more time together. That doesn't have to be face-to-face. Time together can be on the phone, via E-mail, writing letters, anything that keeps the flow of communication going between the two of you. Check with them to ascertain how best to stay in touch.

Then let them know how they impact you. Often we don't take the time to let those close to us know what their insights do for us. A friend of mine decided to start a "compliment of the week" campaign. She was going to pay a compliment to someone close to her at least once a week. At first people wondered what she was up to, but after a while they just accepted that she was getting more perceptive! Let them know you appreciate them.

Relationships can be redefined. You can both decide you want more out of the relationship. Maybe she, too, would like your input, support, ideas, or challenges. Approach her and ask if this could be a collaborative effort on both your parts. Find out what she'd like to work on and then offer to play that role.

My last suggestion is occasionally just to sidestep the goal achievement and take the time to do nothing but have fun together, even if you E-mail jokes to each other or send funny postcards. Make your relationship a fun buddy. Both of you will benefit.

Since one small group of people can't fulfill all your needs, you can create special groups for specific needs. I'm very fortunate to belong to three groups that fill a big place in my life. Each is career linked but not necessarily career focused. Each serves its own unique purpose. One is large, thirty-eight hundred people; another is small, twenty people; and the third is even smaller, a handful of close colleagues and friends.

First is my industry association, the National Speakers Association (NSA). I joined this group in 1976 when I was just entering professional speaking, and they had about two hundred members at the time. I've seen NSA grow to thirty-eight hundred members with thirty-nine chapters and their own international conference center. In 1976 when I joined, I knew very little about this business, so I attended, listened to, and read virtually everything they produced. Since the association was small, I had personal access to everyone. Then as NSA and I grew, I served on some committees, took on various chairmanships, and ultimately ran for the board of directors. In 1989 I was the national president and had more fun while getting more done than any time I can remember.

NSA provided me a forum for exploring ideas and a vehicle for personal growth. It let me see the best and brightest in my field and also some who weren't. I was able to talk with the veterans, learn from the experts, avoid mistakes others had made, and build lifelong friendships. NSA shortened my learning curve by several years. Now what about your field? What are the associations or societies in your field? How can you tap into them? When you join your industry association, you can work with the shakers and movers of your profession to advance the business for all. In doing so you also advance yourself and build a reputation as one who is involved, concerned, and committed to the profession. You will make more vital friendships than you can imagine.

The second organization I'm part of is Speakers Roundtable. This is a group of twenty of the most popular and successful speakers in the world. They are veterans, each of whom has delivered more than a thousand professional speeches, has earned several million dollars in speaking fees, and has been recognized as a leader in his or her field. Collectively they're the authors of scores of top-selling books, tapes, and video programs. Some of the members own businesses doing more than $50 million a year, and some operate independently out of their homes. Their ages range from thirty-six to eighty-nine, and their breadth of experience is enormous. This is an invitation-only group that has existed since the 1960s.

We get together two times a year, once in the summer for four days at a resort; this is half business and half social with our spouses, and we spend the full four days looking for ways to help and learn from one another. In the winter, we have a three-day meeting where we bring in speech and acting coaches to fine-tune our presentations. Imagine multimillionaires and octogenarians speaking before and being critiqued by their peers and a speaking coach every year. The value is immeasurable. What an experience! I'm honored to have been invited into this wonderful group. Within this group I have intimate friendships in which I can reveal my finances, my goals, and my fears and in every case have someone who is very capable of helping me. Though our businesses sometimes compete, we don't consider ourselves competitors. We heartily encourage clients to choose whomever they like best. Next time the business will come to us.

Build Your Own Roundtable

My point is that you, too, can have a roundtable for your own field. Find a handful of people who are at or just above your level of achievement. Make sure they are eager to grow and willing to help others grow. Assure them that they're each bringing a unique and valuable skill to the group. Be very selective and admit only people who can admire one another; no room for leaners here. Meet once a year at first and help each other grow. Limit the rules: Don't have any reports at first, just let this be fun, don't do committee work. I'll guarantee you it will be one of the greatest resources you can build. Learn as you go. Don't try to structure it too much.

The third group I enjoy is not really a formal group at all but just a handful of good friends who are in the same business. You might think these good friends should be in my inner circle. But actually we don't have that consistent or frequent contact. These are colleagues with whom I have only occasional contact, so I'd put them in the outer circle. But at the same time they are people I greatly respect and enjoy being with.

In this group we do business with one another sometimes, we pass along referrals, we coordinate our travel so we can occasionally create minivacations together. This collegiality is great fun, but at the same time it's directly beneficial to our careers. We're one another's best cheerleaders, our kindest and most honest critics, and social friends.

How could you create circles like these in your life? It starts with just two people of like mind, and it builds from there. Soon, you may wish to build other groups for different purposes in your life. The steps are generally the same—just start the connections and follow the natural path of what emerges. There's no telling what you may someday create. My fellow Speakers Roundtable member, Charles "Tremendous" Jones, says, "Five years from now you will be the same person you are today except for two things: the books you read and the people you meet." Why not determine whom and how you want to meet so that you mold your own future?

Author James Newton shares an example of his close group of "uncommon friends." As a young man he befriended a circle of people who literally changed the world! His circle of colleagues and closest friends included Thomas Edison, Dr. Alexis Carrel, Charles Lindbergh, Harvey Firestone, and Henry Ford. I challenge anyone to top that as an example of choosing your friends well. As their lives advanced, so did Jim Newton's. He had opportunities beyond his wildest dreams just because of whom he associated with. The learners of today will be the leaders of tomorrow, so look around you for people who are eager to grow and see how you can help them as they help you. Connect with them and build some alliances with people who will help you grow. Again, set your standards high. Choose people who you can tell will have a bright future and with whom you can relate as an equal as you grow. Who knows, one plus one might equal one thousand!

Your relationships are an integral part of your life, and they can help to nurture your nature. Your nature plus your resources equals your future potential. And that future can be unlimited.

THOUGHT BREAK
- Who are in your inner circle?
- What role do they play in your life?
- What role do you play in theirs?
- How do they complement you, balance you?
- Whom do you need in your inner circle? What might be missing?
- How will you go about attracting those relationships to you?

13. Your Search for Meaning: Outside and Inside

Why?

This may be the most compelling word of all. The answer to it gives meaning to whatever preceded it. Children ask why of everything. Parents pretend to know the answers. Both of them are piqued to find out why.

The reason why is so important in human thought is that thought revolves around meaning. If something has no meaning to us, we ignore it. When it takes on meaning, we fix our attention on it. Take a moment now to look up from this book and scan the area around you for sights and sounds. What do you notice? Why did you notice it?

As I just paused, I heard a siren. It was an emergency vehicle with two lifeguards in it from the beach nearby. You could say I noticed it because of the loudness and motion, but I've seen people in New York City and Paris sit calmly by while surrounded by such actions and sounds. We attend to the things that have meaning to us.

Once I saw that the siren was for a beach emergency, my attention moved on to the people sitting nearby in the restaurant where I am writing this. The siren wasn't immediately meaningful to my situation.

If that same siren had been a fire truck's, I might have searched for an exit route or scanned the building for smoke to ensure that the "bell" didn't toll for me.

Again, what did you notice? Why?

Think of a typical day for you, perhaps yesterday. What did you do? Why? Seek to define the meaning each activity had for you.

Why do we brush our teeth? Habit? No, we do so in order to have fresh breath and to retain our healthy teeth. Why go to work? Money? Sure, but also to attain a sense of usefulness, to have something meaningful to do. Study after study reveals that people's primary motivation for work is to have something worthwhile to do. Ask very old people who are still vital and alert, "What is the key to long life?" Quite often they'll say, "Always have something to look forward to."

Without meaning, depression sets in. Without meaning, we don't feel alive.

That's why it is so valuable to set goals for yourself, especially goals that involve doing things that serve others. When we have a goal on which to focus, our life tends to reorganize itself around making it happen. The resources, solutions, and answers start to appear.

Sam and Laura

Down deep, somewhere inside you, you know what you are designed to do. There is a voice, a feeling, a sixth sense that tells you. Ever since you were a child you have had a sense of destiny, the feeling that things would unfold in a particular direction.

This "knowledge" has wavered from time to time and may have been almost forgotten, but it is not quite gone. It is still there today, waiting to guide you.

Sam was only eight years old when he declared to his family that he would become an astronaut. Pretty ambitious considering his working-class family and lack of connections. Yet he persisted in his endeavor. His toys were rockets and airplanes. He excelled in school and later signed up for Air Force ROTC.

All were impressed but few surprised when he was chosen valedictorian of his suburban high school graduating class.

Amazingly, he received appointments to both the Air Force Academy and West Point. Of course he chose the Academy and went to Colorado Springs, where he graduated with a degree in astronautical engineering.

Sam has a strategic thinking bandwidth, high commitment, knowledge and empathy values, is math, picture, and body smart, had a supportive background, a director style, and high velocity. He is very well suited to the path he has chosen. With no head start he really needed that high velocity to sustain his advancement.

First he became a pilot, then an instructor, then an instructor of the instructor pilots. He flew jets and loved it. After a short tour flying C-130s in Europe, he faced a choice. The military was downsizing. He was a captain. Should he continue his military career toward astronaut or . . . ?

He chose early retirement and today is a commercial pilot with a promising career, a beautiful family, and a happy life. An astronaut? No. But a man who is enjoying life and continuing to learn and grow.

At age eight, something inside him connected with jets and freedom and altitude. On some level he knew what he loved and wanted to do. His eight-year-old mind focused on the most visible media image, the astronaut. As he approached his goal, he changed his role, not a cop-out but a redirection.

Notice that he went from a total ignorance about flying to become a world traveler with a career as a pilot and a degree in his field. Notice also that he excelled as a student, a citizen, and a father. He is living a much larger life than he would have without the initial goal to become an astronaut. And I'll bet his quality of life is even better than if he had single-mindedly stayed committed to astronaut. For others, the original goal would be the best, but for Sam another direction was a better fit. I'd call that success. How about you?

Laura first attended Mass at age five. Her mom had recently become a Catholic. When Laura inquired about the church, her mom said, "This is where Jesus lives."

At the end of the service, Laura said, "I want to see Jesus." Her mom tried to explain, but the five-year-old didn't get it. Finally, her mom said, "That's enough, Laura, let's go home." Laura resisted. Mom insisted. Then Laura bolted across the aisle and bear-hugged a marble post. She yelled out, for all to hear, "I'm not leaving till I see Jesus!"

Her mother was humiliated. The more she asserted, the louder Laura protested. Finally the priest came over, bent down, took Laura by the hand, and gently led her to the altar where he showed her the Sacraments. After a couple of minutes Laura returned happily to her mom, content to go home.

That was twenty years ago. Today we call Laura, Sister Laura. She became a nun! In that role she has excelled in school and thrived as a servant to others. I guess we'd have to concede that she "saw Jesus."

Laura is an operational thinker, who has high commitment and empathy values, is body and people smart, with a marginally supportive background. Her behavioral style is director, and her velocity is moderate. With the exception of her director style, which is not a major factor in her assignment, Laura's profile is just right for her chosen role.

Where did her clarity come from? How could a five-year-old possibly know her life's calling? And why don't most people have the clarity of purpose that touched Laura and Sam? How come some of us get into our sixties without ever having a clear purpose?

I believe that all of us "know" our calling. We just fail to *notice*. Marsha Sinetar wrote a book titled *Do What You Love, The Money Will Follow.* In my experience that's true. Things may not turn out as we originally hoped or expected, but the path is worth following.

Our interests and impulses are messages we ought to listen to. The potentials within us are naturally drawn to that which will fulfill them. As Emerson said, "*Desire* is possibility seeking expression." So if something fascinates or fulfills you, you really ought to take notice. Your natural path may be calling you. There is fulfillment in ordinary living.

Dymaxion Thinking

R. Buckminster Fuller, called by some the Leonardo da Vinci of the twentieth century, was an inventor, engineer, architect, poet, philosopher, scientist, and more. He coined the term *dymaxion*. It means, simply, maximum performance with minimum materials—doing more with less.

This concept is present in his creations, such as the strong yet lightweight geodesic dome, the most prominent of which sits at the entrance of Disney's EPCOT Center in Florida. Another application is the World Energy Grid, a plan for the linking of all the world's renewable energy sources to produce abundant electricity affordably for all major population centers on earth indefinitely.

Fuller's goal was to find ways to make the world work for 100 percent of humanity in the shortest possible time through spontaneous cooperation without ecological damage or disadvantage to anyone. Today, Fuller's work is being carried on by Peter Meisen, a friend of mine who formed Global Energy Network Institute (GENI) in 1986. This nonprofit effort has led Peter around the world and caused him to meet and collaborate with numerous world leaders.

As a result of Peter's quest to open the global mind to this cooperative venture, former adversaries have laid down their arms while laying electrical cables to replace them.

This has resulted in linking energy sources across borders and time zones to provide inexpensive, off-peak energy production to areas that most need it. It's easy to see the effect this can have on world peace. You don't bomb your own energy plants, nor do you terrorize places where you have branch offices.

Peter Meisen was a young man with an engineering background and a profound personal concern for the world's welfare.

He did not know "the right people" or have access to a large trust fund when he started GENI. He didn't have the language skills, knowledge of diplomacy and protocol, or a position of scientific prominence. He wasn't one of the top authorities on his topic. He merely had a sincere desire to make a difference.

By choosing this path, Peter Meisen had also committed himself to a life of personal growth. Like Walt Disney when he was a cartoonist dreaming of Disneyland, Peter's goal was bigger than Peter. If he didn't grow, the goal wouldn't show.

So Peter began to identify his own strengths and find people with differing abilities. He sought connections with anyone who could, even temporarily, become excited about his goals. He built alliances, helped others, sought mentors, and grew a root system (resource network) of enormous proportions.

He is a voracious student in his field, but he doesn't try to master everything. He respects and aligns with the strengths and passions in others. And the Global Energy Network* is rapidly becoming a reality.

The official ending of the Cold War was the destruction of the Berlin Wall in 1989 after forty years of tension and missiles pointed at each other. Two months later, East and West Germany began the interconnection of their electrical grids because it made such good economic sense. When King Hussein of Jordan and Yitzhak Rabin of Israel signed the Washington Declaration for peace, the first two infrastructure projects included the interconnection of telephone lines and power grids. The geographic distance was small, and the technology had existed for years. It just took diplomacy and mutual economic benefit to enable the engineers to build a physical link that will help both countries. Today, many former enemies are following suit: Chile and Argentina, Turkey and Iran, India and Pakistan. If these nations can move from conflict to cooperation, so can they all.

Now back to the person behind all of this. Based on what I

* For information on his work, contact Peter Meisen at GENI, World Trade Center, 1250 Sixth Avenue, Suite 901, San Diego, CA 92101 (619) 595-0139.

have just told you about him, do an Acorn Profile of Peter
Meisen. The clues are all there. What are his highest values? How
do you know? What is his velocity? Has his background seemed
to help or not? What are his greatest smarts? What is his bandwidth? His behavioral style? Write out your answers before reading more. See how well you are *noticing more.*

Peter's velocity is very high. He has taken on the biggest of all
causes, saving the world. His commitment and empathy values
are so high they are off the chart. He also has a high knowledge
value. His wealth value is relatively low. His background is neutral. His smarts are picture, math/logic, and people smarts. He
has a conceptual bandwidth. I didn't give you enough information to know his behavioral style; it is director. Look back over
the description of Peter and link these observations to the information available to you.

With his profile it is fairly easy to see how his current role provides the meaning and purpose that suit him. Our ideas of what
is or is not meaningful are usually an outgrowth of our Acorn
Profile. We are drawn toward that for which we are well suited.
"Desire is possibility seeking fulfillment."

You are like Peter Meisen in many ways. Though your profile
may be very different from his, there are things you are greatly
concerned about. You possess strengths that, once matched with
others, could really make a difference in your company, community, or world. You contain the seeds of a forest of mighty oaks.

The key to tapping this growth potential is beginning the
process. Take the first steps; act on your impulses. Find ways to
enhance the world through your actions. Don't start by looking
at yourself; start by looking around you. What are you concerned about? How would you change the world if you could?

Growth doesn't occur without reaching out. Reaching out to
help stimulates a simultaneous outreach for resources—branches
and roots. As you need them, somehow the resources seem happily to appear. Not always where you suspected they would be,
but there nonetheless.

Your job is not fully to understand the world but simply to enhance it. Make it better because you were here—whether that be through an entertaining performance, a beautiful sculpture, a simpler solution, a kind gesture, or a global movement. Grow where you are planted and branch out to connect with and serve the world.

Where Do You Look—Inside or Outside?

Goals that involve *getting* can be very powerful. Sam's goal of becoming an astronaut led him to travel the world and transcend his former limits. Laura's goal led her to true spiritual happiness. My own goal of becoming an authority on personal growth led me to transform my limited life and vastly expand my horizons. In many ways, you have done the same over the years. Notice it.

Goals that involve *giving* can be even more powerful. When we connect with a cause outside of ourselves, we have more of an influence on others. Think of the best known businesses that did this. GENI was formed in order to give adequate energy to all people in order to meet their living needs. Apple Computer was founded with the goal of making technology work for everyone. Ford Motor Company built cars that the average person could afford and use. Disneyland was created to become "the happiest place on earth." The *New York Times* informs us daily with "all the news that's fit to print." The great insurance companies began as a way for people to share the expense and reduce the impact of loss or disaster.

The movement that has revolved around Mother Teresa's ministry grew out of her intense desire to help "the poorest of the poor." In every case, an impulse to give or to get gave meaning to those involved.

Look around you again—what do you care about? What would you change? Look wider. Examine your daily life, your community, your family, your business. What are you concerned about? What would you change?

Maybe you can change things for the better. Maybe the seeds

of a greater contribution already live within you. Write down your thoughts. Notice what excites or bothers you. Think about it. Think beyond it to a better condition. How could you initiate some actions that would grow new possibilities for those affected?

Grow where you are planted. Then branch out toward even more . . . toward meaning.

Meaning and Fulfillment

"What's nice," Walt Disney said to his friend and coworker, Mike Vance, "is to be grown-ups like we are . . . and to remember the kids we were back then." Then he asked Mike, "Do you know what's even nicer than that? It is to be grown-ups like we are, remember the kids we once were, and to know that we have become the person that, as a child, we hoped and dreamed, someday we might become.

"That's called *fulfillment* and it's something every human being dreams to achieve."

A few years ago I read a newspaper headline that said, "Workers want jobs that fit their values and talents." The article described how, despite layoffs, downsizing, and corporate mergers, workers surveyed were more concerned about job satisfaction than mere job security.

Study after study cites pay as one of the lesser motivators, assuming, of course, that the pay is fair and dependable. The elements that spark initiative and generate job satisfaction, at all levels, are meaningful work, responsibility for one's own actions/results, appreciation of one's contributions, and respect for one's opinion. Out of that grows health, relationships, continual learning, and the willingness to exert initiative, to bring a sense of ownership to one's work.

Fulfillment results when an acorn becomes an oak, a nurturer becomes a nurse, an explorer pursues a quest, or a message finds its medium. You and I experience fulfillment whenever we are making a difference. If we are doing something that matters in some way, we tend to smile inside. And this shows up in the quality of our work.

You'd think that one of the most stressful jobs on earth would be air traffic controller, juggling takeoff and landing patterns with hundreds of lives at stake. Granted, that can be truly stressful. But in the evaluation of most stressful occupations, guess what comes in as even more stressful? Toll booth operator.

This seems to defy logic, but only if you think in terms of the actions and the thinking required. What makes the toll booth so stressful is not the work but the lack of meaning. A machine could do this job . . . and probably should.

We need to know that what we do counts. We need work that fits our values and talents, something for which we are suited. If we don't find meaning in the job itself, we must bring meaning to it through the way we approach it.

The toll collector who sets a goal to make each person smile as he or she pays the toll actually transforms the job into a cause or mission. Conversely, the air traffic controller who simply does the work, with no thought of the people involved, will likely gain very little fulfillment from his or her work.

THOUGHT BREAK

What do you find fulfilling? Here is a quick questionnaire to help you isolate the elements that lie along your natural path to fulfillment.

- When was the last time you got caught up in your actions or thoughts and lost track of time?
- What do you like to do for people?
- What has been the work you've most enjoyed over the years?
- When was a time you felt fully alive?
- Describe your idea of the perfect job.
- Whom do you admire and why?

Take a little time now and write out your answers to these questions. Then look over your answers for patterns. Search for common themes or traits that seem to stand out. Most likely, there will be a strong similarity among your responses.

Fulfillment comes when we spend our energies on what we care about, believe in, and have talent for. Psychologist William Glasser said, "If a job utilizes talents, appeals to interests, and relates to values, it will be fulfilling." The wonderful diversity within people allows for endless combinations of pursuits each of which satisfies someone.

Want a happy life? Want advancement in your career? Want better relationships? Want to make a difference in the world? Then follow your nature. The more constructive activity there is in your life, the more satisfied and happy you're going to be. Conversely, the less active you are, the more depressed and lonely you become. A human is a purpose-driven social animal. We need to connect with people, not just be surrounded by them. We need goals and things to do and people to do them with or for. It's not optional.

One time I was in Minnesota doing a training program for a financial services company. At the end of the program a man asked me if he could drive me back to my hotel, and I said okay. Along the way he said, "Jim, what do you think about my being an estate planner?"

"What do you mean?"

"Well, I'm sixty-five years old, I just retired from the military recently, I've got my pension, and I've gone into estate planning. I'd just like to know what you think about it. Do you think it's a good choice?"

"Frankly, I don't know enough about you to know if that's a good choice, but how do you feel about it?"

"Well," he said, "I feel good about it."

"Do you feel like you're doing an honorable thing," I asked. He said yes.

Then I asked, "Does this excite you? Do you get a sense of real self-respect for what you're doing?"

"No."

"Well, how long do you think you're going to do this?"

"I don't know, eight or ten years."

"So you do this for eight or ten years, then what will you do?"

"I guess I'll retire," he replied.

"Okay, then what will you do when you retire?"

"Well, I'll do whatever I want to do. I mean, I'll play golf, I'll fish, I'll travel."

"It doesn't sound like that's very clear in your mind."

"No, but that's what I'm going to do."

"And how long do you figure you'll retire?" I asked.

"Oh, maybe another eight or ten years."

"So then what are you going to do?"

"Then, I guess, I'll die," he said.

I said, "You don't seem to be particularly happy about that."

"Well, I'm not. Would you be?"

"No, but why are you planning for it?"

"Excuse me?" he asked.

"You just laid out your plan. You've got a twenty-year plan, eight or ten years you're going to be an estate planner, eight or ten years you're going to retire, then you're out of here."

"Well, I don't . . . I . . . I guess you're right," he said.

His lack of purpose was obvious. He had no meaningful goals, and his quality of life reflected it. Was he living life fully? No. He needed to determine what he truly cared about and then do it.

People need purpose. When we're not planning toward something, our life starts to diminish, it starts to shrink. There are many examples of the fact that the more purpose we have in our life, the longer we live.

Look at the example of Colonel Harland Sanders. Harland Sanders at age sixty-five took his first Social Security check and started the Kentucky Fried Chicken empire. When he retired, if you could call it that, he was much past age sixty-five and a multimillionaire to boot.

We need a purpose, some reason to get out of bed in the morning, something to challenge us. Brain research has shown that if we keep ourselves intellectually challenged and stimulate the mind, we may actually cause brain cells, called neurons, to branch wildly and establish new connections. We create more dendritic tissue. So stimulate your brain with a purpose and challenge your thinking!

We have to have a purpose, because it's the source of the life energy that makes our lives meaningful. Setting goals is so important because it gives us a purpose to live. That's why people say you've got to have a dream or a vision.

But interestingly, purpose doesn't come from outside us; it always comes from inside, and it goes out toward others as some form of service or self-expression.

Are you living the life you were meant to live?

When you identify the big purpose that you want to go after for a certain portion of your life, all of a sudden the life energy you need starts coming in to you to fulfill that purpose.

And you can do this at any age! How much you have lived doesn't have anything to do with this. Look at examples of people who started when they were young with a clear purpose, or people who started much later in life, like Grandma Moses, who started painting at age seventy-eight and continued well into her nineties.

Look at Henry Ford. Now here's a guy who revolutionized the way human beings live on this earth by the invention and proliferation of the automobile. Henry Ford didn't even produce his first car until after age forty-five. His purpose wasn't expressed until the last half of his life.

Norman Vincent Peale had a brilliant life, and he died with a smile on his face at age ninety-five on Christmas Eve. Norman Vincent Peale wrote the book that made his career, *The Power of Positive Thinking,* at age fifty-three.

Mother Teresa lived a long and abundant life serving the poorest of the poor. As a young woman she identified her purpose and ever since then dedicated herself to it.

My dear friend the late Cavett Robert, founder of the National Speakers Association, gave his *first* paid speech at age sixty-one. He continued to speak professionally for more than twenty-five years.

Winston Churchill was a troubled youth, but he went on in his later years to rescue England from its darkest days by providing the kind of leadership that inspired us all.

We often need a cause larger than our skills in order to grow. Thinking big is allowed and, in fact, encouraged!

When was a time that you felt really alive? I asked this question recently and one woman said, "When I was on a hiking and biking tour of Canada." I asked her what was unique about that. She said it was not only a beautiful and exciting experience but also a challenging time requiring her to stretch and to do some things that she wasn't quite sure she could do. Maybe for you it was a rafting trip, or singing in a huge choir, or being president of your industry association, chair of a convention, working on a political campaign, or a major activity that made you feel really alive.

I remember a few years ago when I was chosen to be the keynote speaker for the National Speakers Association. The convention that year was in Dallas, and I was addressing an audience of sixteen hundred professional speakers including all the best of my peers. That challenge of addressing my colleagues in a one-hour general session at their annual meeting caused me to come up with new ideas, new materials, and a new level of performance that I'd never shown before. I was at my best at that moment. Not the best I would ever be, just the best I could realistically aspire to be in that situation at that time in my life.

The same is true for you, if you'll remember that the last time you felt really alive—a time when you were doing something that stretched your abilities and sharpened your skills, when your mind and body were very active. Your purpose or goal no doubt tested you and made you greater than you had been before. Only then did you feel fully alive. When there is a reason to grow, there is room to grow and a natural path to follow.

14. Identifying Your Psychological Blind Spots

Albert Einstein said that the hardest part of discovering the theory of relativity was determining how to think about it. Do you often think about thinking? Probably not. Thinking is something we do automatically, outside our awareness of how we are doing it. We don't "think" about thinking. Our brain just does its job somehow and keeps on thinking. In fact, it's been said that our brain is capable of more thought patterns than the number of atoms in the entire universe.

Everything humans have ever achieved started with just one thought, so thinking is obviously the most productive activity of all. Let's explore the nature of your thinking.

Those who have mastered the art of thinking are the ones who have shaped the world. I use the word *art* intentionally because thought is much more of a process of *expression* than one of *control*. Consider this: Have you ever tried to control your thinking? Maybe you woke up one morning and thought, *I will think only happy thoughts today!* Did that happen? Probably not. Or if you thought, *I will think only of my main priority today. I do not want any unrelated thoughts today.* Could that happen? No, probably not.

Thinking is very chaotic. The neurons in your brain fire at a speed of a hundred million billion times per second and make connections randomly with past experiences and present information all the time trying to adapt to the current environment or the current challenge. You can try to focus, but that's really only directing the *application* of your thinking.

Yet to direct the application of your thinking can yield wonderful results. This is where the chaos of thinking becomes efficient. We can focus the application of our thinking in three ways. First, we can focus on a goal, an objective. Second, we can focus with words. Third, we can focus by using a model.

The first way is important because our thoughts require a nucleus, a magnet around which they can organize to produce a desired result. That's why goal setting is so critical to personal or organizational growth. The goal gives a focal point to the thinking of everyone who's involved.

By focusing on a goal, we clear away all other options. Author Mihaly Csikszentmihalyi says that focused thinking is the key to achieving our potential. When you have a goal and focus on it, your energy can become focused, and the options, the path, to achieve the goal become clear. Think of how a potted plant near a window always grows toward the light. It finds a path to what it wants. That's what happens when you focus your thinking. Once the goal becomes clear, so do the options and decisions.

Words are another way we can apply our thinking. Words work in much the same way as the act of focusing. Words help us target our thinking and describe and categorize our impressions. Words help us apply our thinking by making quicker connections to our thoughts.

If you have a large vocabulary, you have thousands of ways to remember and describe things. Until we find words to describe our impressions of the world, we're limited in our ability to think about them. If I tell you I have a dog, what kind of animal do you picture in your thoughts? Now, what if I say I have a St. Bernard puppy? The better the picture I can create through words, the more accurate the image will be in other people's minds as they think about it. There may be a million St. Bernards in the world, each in many ways different from the others. But one thing they all share is the quality of being a St. Bernard and not a poodle or a hound. This book has given you a new vocabulary for self-awareness, new terms to use when learning about people and communicating with them.

The third way to control the application of your thinking is with models. A model is a replica of something, an incomplete representation. Models, even though incomplete, help us to understand a larger concept or help us make a mental connection, thus helping us to think more effectively.

For example, in astronomy we speak of constellations, galaxies, and solar systems to organize a multitude of celestial information. The stars themselves may not have any actual relationship to one another, but the constellation model helps us in thinking about them.

Likewise, psychology is a way of using models to think about the various systems within people. We speak of concepts such as personality, reasoning, emotion, intellect, and values. We refer to these things as if they were tangible reality when in fact they are just models we use to understand and describe the chaotic diversity within individual human beings. You and I may be the same age, the same sex, and have the same IQ. We may have grown up with the same parents and siblings, gone to the same schools, and made the same score on our Scholastic Aptitude Test. But we would still be so unique and diverse in other ways that no one who knew us would ever think we were the same person. There are always exceptions to our ways of describing our world, but models still serve us very well as thinking tools. The better my model is at describing my concept, the better others can think about it as I do.

In this book I've described many models, each with its own area of application. These models are based upon years of exploration and testing against other models for reliability. But even with all this validation, they're still incomplete. You see, in most cases it isn't practical to try to be perfect about something. I'd much rather see you take these ideas as just tools and put them to use in making your life more productive and satisfying, rather than trying to make them perfect or waiting until they're clinically validated or totally reliable. I believe that ideas, like people, are works in process. Let these models and tools clarify your thoughts and help you create the life you desire.

Remember that I said Albert Einstein stated that the hardest part of discovering the theory of relativity was determining how to think about it? To reach his breakthrough he chose to create a new mental model, because he couldn't solve the problem with the old model. So he devised a mental model of himself riding on a beam of light as if it were a motorcycle at 186,000 miles per second. Really! Of course that model is ridiculously unrealistic, but it served his purposes well, providing him with a way of thinking about things he had never considered before, and it yielded one of the greatest breakthroughs of modern science, the theory of relativity.

By the way, once that idea or model served its purpose, it was no longer needed. Einstein simply moved on to other ways of thinking and higher levels of understanding.

The vision of a flat earth served our ancestors well enough until they discovered that the earth was round and started to lengthen their travels. The vision of earth as the center of the universe made good sense until we discovered our solar system, the Milky Way galaxy, and more. Each model assisted our thinking to reach the next level of thinking and understanding. There's no telling how much we still don't know, but that's all right, because everybody's in the same situation. It's like Will Rogers said: "Everyone's ignorant, just on different subjects."

We've known for years Newton's law that for every action there is an equal and opposite reaction. Well, here's Cathcart's corollary: For everything you know, on that same subject there is an equal or greater amount that you don't know. It is said that one weekday edition of the *New York Times* contains more diverse information than our great-grandparents were exposed to in their lifetime. So how do we know what we know? Where do we get our information?

Some time ago I joined an organization that I'm impressed with, called the Institute of Noetic Sciences. Noetic science in this sense means the study of knowing: How do people know what they know? How do they get the information? How do they store and use the information? How do they give it meaning? Where do you get your information? There are two models I'll give you that fit nicely together. One is called information filters; the other I call the six sources of truth.

To understand our information filters, picture yourself standing at the edge of a small pond. Drop one small pebble into the pond and picture four concentric circles form as ripples on the pond from where you dropped the pebble. But in this case, the ripples come in toward you rather than going out from you.

These four circles represent your information filters, how you receive and retain information.

The outer circle represents exposure, all that you've been exposed to, your total life's experience. No matter how active, well read, or well traveled you've been, there are many limits to what you've seen and experienced, so this circle represents just the part of the world that you've been exposed to. Going inward, the next circle is attention, what you paid attention to as you journeyed through this exposure. Many things would not have

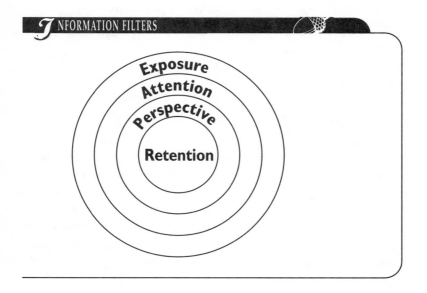

entered your perception because you weren't paying attention to them as they occurred.

The next circle is called perspective or point of view. The way you look at things further limits how much of them you perceive or what aspect of them you perceive. For example, your values and beliefs can color what you notice in most any situation. Say you believe that all homeless people are lazy—then anything you hear from someone who's homeless you will discount because you don't respect the person who's saying it. The fact of the matter is, the only thing that's true about all homeless people is that they're homeless. For all you know, they may be brilliant and hardworking, just having a tough go of it.

The innermost circle is called retention or memory. Memory is notoriously selective. To prove this to yourself, sit down with some of your family members and take turns describing a situation from your past. Ask each person to describe his or her memory of the situation. Then notice how different each person's memories were. Your memory of what you were exposed to selects how much of it you really know.

Studies on listening have found that we retain only about 25 percent of what we hear twenty-four hours after we've heard it. So we need better systems for learning what we already know, better systems for retaining and storing information so that we can recall it more efficiently.

Increase Your Exposure

Here's a way to develop a better system. Using the circles again, look at the model for information filters. If we want to know more, we've got to increase the number of things we're exposed to. We must expose ourselves to more ideas, more experiences, more overall information. Notice when and where the pebble gets dropped in the water. Where does your point of view start? The rest of the pond is still out there, but your exposure to it is limited to one small area.

Notice More

As the ripples move inward toward you, the next ring is attention. We need to pay attention to more things as we're having these experiences and begin to notice more. Look around for more details; notice the patterns in things and people and feelings. My friend Steve Curtis, a creative entrepreneur, says that a good formula for success is: Show up, pay attention, tell the truth, and don't worry about the outcome. An interesting formula! In many instances it would not apply, but as a life strategy it is hard to beat. If you don't show up, nothing happens. If you merely show up but don't pay attention, likewise nothing happens for you. To attend a class is not enough for learning. You must also pay attention, understand, and retain what you heard. Each ring feeds into the next one toward the center, finally resulting in the total of all you know.

See Things from Different Angles

For the ring of perspective we need to shift points of view. Imagine sitting in a window seat on an airplane. As you look out the window, you notice that you are flying over a large city. How much of it do you see? Only the part that is accessible through your limited porthole. But by changing to another seat on the other side of the plane, you double what you can see just by temporarily altering your perspective.

We should try on points of view just like new clothes. Actually, we should have a point of view wardrobe where we try on different points of view from time to time and look at things in different ways. That's because the more ways we can see something, the more elements of it we will perceive. The fewer ways we see things, the more psychological blind spots we will have.

What's going on in your mind? Can you switch to a different point of view, or are you rigidly locked in to only one? Can you stretch your point of view? Try it.

For example, try this exercise: Is a person fully responsible for what he or she does? Answer from your usual point of view, then discuss it from a totally different point of view. Try debating it with a friend. First debate the pro position, then switch sides and debate the con position.

Increase Your Retention

Now move inward one more circle and work on expanding your retention. Work on your memory skills. You can improve your skills for storing, sorting, and categorizing information so that you retain a great deal more of it. To do this, try taking a memory course or developing a database of what you know on a subject. The more you notice, the more you know.

The more you are exposed to, the more you can potentially learn and know. The more you pay attention to, the more you can understand. The more you shift to varying points of view, the more *thoroughly* you can understand. The more you can recall and retain, the more you will be able to use when you need it.

Everything you know or suspect to be true is based on the limited amount of varied information that has come through those four filters.

Sources of Truth

Also everything you know has come to you from one or more of six basic sources that I call the six sources of truth. They were inspired by the work of Hunter Lewis as described in the book *A Question of Values*.

To understand these six sources, I'd like you to picture yourself out on a walk in the mountains. It's a beautiful day, clear blue sky, with wispy, white clouds. It's a pleasant temperature. You don't even need a jacket. You're out alone because your partner stayed back at the cabin to relax and read a book. But you wanted to be outdoors and enjoy nature.

You cross a stream and smile as a few young people pass you

coming from the opposite direction. You keep walking farther. You stop to watch squirrels play and to watch an eagle soar over a canyon. You are very happy.

You've lost track of time, and in fact you didn't even notice that a large black cloud is now overhead. You feel the wind picking up. It's cooled, and you wish you'd brought your jacket. Suddenly, sharp rain pelts down and the wind gusts all around you. You look around, but you can't remember which way you came from. You start to panic. You need to take cover, and if the rain gets any harder, you'll need to find shelter.

You find yourself at a multiple crossroads and don't know which road to take.

Now your life may be on the line. It could get dark and the storm could get stronger. You've got to get off the mountain quickly. You know that choosing the wrong road could take you farther from your destination, and without protection you could get hypothermia and possibly die. You didn't come prepared for a storm! You just wanted to enjoy a beautiful day!

There are six different roads at the juncture. But you can choose only one. Each road leads you to one source of information, one type of solution that you can use to escape from the threats around you. So which of the following sources would you choose, which road would you take?

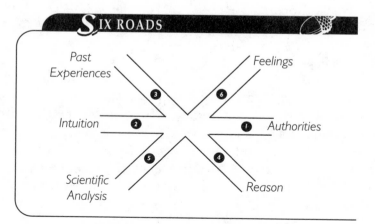

Would you take road number 1? On this road you would find authorities and expert sources. You would find people, books, experts, leaders, teachers, textbooks, reference manuals, encyclopedias, news agencies, and official sources of all types. Anyone you would want advice from, from world leaders to people out of history, resides along this path. These authorities would tell you how to survive the storm and how to get back to the cabin. **By choosing this road you entrust your welfare to others. Their guidance will determine your fate. How do you feel about that?**

Would you take road number 2? This road would put you in touch with your intuition—inner knowing, personal insight, ahas, epiphanies, eurekas, knowledge that you can't explain. A different knowing that follows an inner trust will be found along this road. **This choice puts your fate in your own hands entirely. How much do you trust your own intuition?**

Maybe you'd prefer to take road number 3. This is the path of your past experience; it leads you through all that you've ever experienced, discovered, seen, heard, or touched with your own hands. If you prefer to trust only that which you've discovered and felt, you may prefer this road. **On this road you would be able to retrace your steps, but what if the path you came on wasn't the safest one for your return?**

Road number 4 appeals to those who like to reason, to really think things through. On this road you'll use all your logic and reasoning ability to examine all sides of the situation and follow a thoughtful path to your solutions. You prefer to sideline your emotions and stick to the most logical solution. Is this the road for you? **Sometimes logic makes great sense, and sometimes senses make the better logic. Which is better this time?**

Road number 5 is the scientific road. This is the road of systematic analysis. It employs testing, analysis, experimentation, and the use of all known laws of science. Do you think this road is the best? **Will you have time to do a thorough analysis and still survive?**

And road number 6 is ruled by feelings. You check your physical sensations at the time. As you walk here you'll follow your gut. You are aware of your fear or dread and move away from it. You sense which direction gives you energy and move toward it. You sense whether the rain is increasing or decreasing. You are very aware of your sensations. **How about it? Are you willing to follow your gut to your survival or demise?**

Remember that your situation in this case could be life-threatening, so the road you choose really counts.

Here are the sources again: authorities, intuition, past experiences, reasoning, scientific analysis, and sensory feelings. Which source would you pursue to find the best answers, the truth? Note the one you chose.

Assuming you did not find your way back on that road, which one would you take next if you had the option? How about the one after that? By choosing your first three roads you have exposed your preferred sources of truth, where you believe the most reliable information will be found.

Ironically, you've also exposed your psychological blind spots. You see, all six roads could lead you to the truth, but which is most reliable varies depending on your situation. One source may be the best now, and another that you value much less could be the best source for you later. Sometimes the best thing you can rely on is your own feelings. Sometimes what you most need to recall is your own experience in relation to something. Other times you should be relying on authority figures or listening to your intuition. Each of these has its place.

The more you learn to listen to messages from all six sources, the better your decisions will be. All six are intertwined on some level, and by pursuing one we may find our answers coming up through another. For example, Thomas Edison would spend countless hours in his lab experimenting and then take catnaps for rest. Many times upon awakening he found that the answers had intuitively popped into his mind. On other occasions he'd pursue a particular path because he just had a feeling it would work out.

Edison's discoveries, like Ben Franklin's and Leonardo da Vinci's before him and Buckminster Fuller's after him, have served humankind in countless ways. Yet he and they used many sources to find the truth. There's a universe of information out there that you and I do not know. If we are to know more, we must begin to notice more. Think about your thinking and allow new mental models to give you insights.

THOUGHT BREAK
- Which sources of truth do you refer to first?
- Do you rely more on outside authorities or inner knowing?
- How will you remind yourself to notice more?
- How can you expose yourself to more information and expand your life experiences?

15. The Fulfillment Grid: Two Things That Determine Your Life

Two old friends of mine once said, "Everyone needs a vehicle for self-development" and "Everyone needs an avenue of self-expression." These were separate statements made at different times. At first, I thought they had both said the same thing. But on closer examination the distinctions are important here. Not only do we need a path to travel so we can express ourselves, but we also need a vehicle, or process, for our own self-development. To develop new skills without a way of using them is frustrating, and to have an opportunity to use a skill you don't yet possess is downright depressing.

Since work takes up so much of our time and physical and mental energy, we often don't seek out hobbies or extracurricular activities to create that avenue for self-expression. So if we don't find that avenue through our work, we remain frustrated. Sometimes our work doesn't allow us to show our true talents. Yet when we make a place in our lives for full self-expression, the payoff is huge!

For example, a friend of mine has a father who was a model employee; he worked forty-two years in a factory without ever taking a sick day. But the work he did there wasn't his outlet for self-expression. His real love was baseball. When he was young, he played in a local league but never tried to go farther because he had to earn a living. Obviously that was before million-dollar sports contracts. But he still expressed himself most fully and effectively through baseball.

On the side, after working from 6 A.M. to 3 P.M., he would coach baseball at the local high school. Then he got an offer to be a scout for a major league team. Besides keeping his regular job, he'd watch about one hundred and twenty games a year, check out the local talent, and let the team know whom it might consider the up-and-comers. It balanced his life and made him a happy man. How do you express your talents and interests at this point in *your* life? The more outlets you can develop, the more fully you can live.

When you have a vehicle for self-development, you ensure that you have a way to grow. Sometimes we grow by the relationships we have in our lives. When someone close to you gives you honest feedback and insights, that input can help you grow, especially if you work to coach each other.

My vehicle for five years was the Junior Chamber of Commerce, the Jaycees. I joined as a charter member of a new chapter in my neighborhood. As one of the first twenty members, it was easy to get elected to offices. I became active in my community, and after each project I'd analyze our successes and failures with the other members. I went on to become a state officer and award winner, then was hired by the national headquarters of the Jaycees to be the manager in charge of individual development programs. My hobby had become my job. It was a wonderful lab for personal improvement.

Though my day job previously was working as a government clerk and held little in the way of individual development, my Jaycees activity helped me to grow by leaps and bounds. All of us need some kind of vehicle for self-development. And then we need an outlet to use that new skill, an avenue for self-expression.

Self-development and self-expression bring me to a model I've been working on for more than fifteen years. I've called it the fulfillment grid, the empowerment grid, and then the mastery grid. Its name is not nearly as important as its use, so let's stick with the fulfillment grid for now.

It is based on two basic elements, *awareness* and *performance*. Self-development comes from the increased *awareness* of where you are right now and learning what is needed in order to grow. And self-expression is how you perform, what you do.

The basic principle of the fulfillment grid is that high awareness multiplied by high performance equals mastery. And mastery yields fulfillment.

Awareness in its simplest form is knowing. Performance in its simplest form is doing. Your entire life is influenced by what you know and what you do. When you change either of these, in some ways you change your life.

So let's start by looking at what you know. Your awareness determines how you think. The more you know about a subject, the more possibilities you can see for it. Throughout this book, I've given you lots of tools to explore your awareness of yourself and others. We've examined your values, your motivation, your perceptions of intelligence. We've looked at behavioral styles and velocity. This certainly affects the possibilities you can see for yourself.

But when you learn only *how* things work, then you're stuck with only processes; you have to do it that way all the time. If you keep on doing what you've always done, you will keep on getting what you've always gotten. The balance of this book is focused on how to use your new awareness to improve your life. It is not enough just to have a solid Acorn Profile. You must also know how to nurture your nature in order to grow continually.

Ralph Waldo Emerson, one of my favorite philosophers, said, "If you learn only methods, you'll be tied to your methods, but if you learn the principles behind the methods, you can devise your own methods."

You might know football coach Vince Lombardi's old line, "Winning's not everything—it's the only thing." Many years after he said that, someone asked him about it and he reportedly said, "I wish I'd never said the thing. What I meant was people should have goals." Many people have picked up one-liners like this and built their whole life around them. I believe that what we need to know is *why* we do what we do. We need to know what we believe in, what we stand for, the purposes behind the processes that we're following. We need to know the principles of how things work. And then we need to apply our performance to our purpose.

The difference between processes and purposes is bridged by principles. If you learn the purposes of why someone is doing something, then you can see which principles apply and which processes make the most sense.

As a child I often enjoyed a TV show called *Watch Mr. Wizard*. A wonderfully friendly, fatherly scientist hosted the show. He would get some kids together in his laboratory and perform the most amazing experiments. In each case, the kids in the studio audience and us kids at home would watch with our mouths open, saying, "Wow, how did he do that?" Then he would explain exactly what he had done and why it worked. He would explain the principles behind the processes.

Once we learned the principles, our awareness expanded and we understood a bit more of why things functioned as they did. Why does the sun rise and set? Why does water boil at a certain temperature? Why does this happen and that happen? Mr. Wizard gave us the principles behind these processes.

Along the same lines, the TV action series *McGuyver* for several years had a very successful run. In each episode, the title character would be stuck in some life-threatening situation, and he would always save the day by figuring out how to apply some simple laws of physics, taking some very common materials and creating just the right tool that would resolve the problem. He took the basic principles of biology, physics, and chemistry and applied them to everyday situations to achieve his goals. Not only were we entertained, we were also educated. We learned something about natural principles.

I truly believe that the person who knows *how* may have a job, but the one who knows *why* will be the boss. When you know purposes, you can make better decisions. The more you're stuck with processes, the harder decisions are.

For example, the purpose of building a business relationship with someone is to secure a customer for life, not just during the process of doing the transaction. The purpose of making a sale is to generate a profitable flow of business, not just to write up a single order. The proper purpose of marrying another person is not just to have a wedding and set up housekeeping, but for the life-enhancing connection that results from that and the impact it has on both parties' lives. Think of the why, and the how will become apparent.

Become aware of the purpose behind every process. Why do you do things in that particular way? Do you do things a certain way because your mother did them that way? Are you blindly following tradition without knowing why? When you ask "why?" you're more purpose driven. When you ask only "how?" you become process driven; you are a slave to the system.

When someone comes to work in my organization, the first thing I want him or her to do is start asking why about everything. Why do we keep the files this way? Why do we keep these records? Why do we contact those people? Why do we go after this segment of the marketplace instead of that segment of it? Why do we offer these products? Why do you give speeches on this subject?

By the way, what is the purpose of filing? The reason I ask this is that most people misunderstand even this simple task. The most common answer I've heard is that filing's purpose is the storage of information. I completely disagree. Filing's purpose is *retrieval* of information! Having something in storage serves no one. Being able to find and access it easily benefits many people.

The more they understand why, the more they can make decisions on their own. If a person knows the reason that something needs to be done but doesn't yet know how to do it, at least he'll fall forward if he makes a mistake. But if a person knows only the steps and doesn't understand the reasons behind them, he must be closely supervised because one bad decision could wreak havoc with the whole system's ability to produce a specific result. As situations change, he's not able to adapt to the change because he doesn't know why he's doing what he's doing.

Let's simplify. *Why* is the purpose. *How* is the process. Which do you focus on most?

Not too long ago I went into a store to buy some gloves. I ride a motorcycle in my spare time, and I wanted to get some lightweight riding gloves for the summer. I went to my usual dealership and found a pair of gloves that I liked, bought them for twenty-two dollars, and took them home. When I tried them on, I discovered they were still a little too hot. I wanted gloves with more ventilation.

So I went back to the dealer and said, "I'd like to trade these gloves for that other pair over there that's more ventilated."

He said, "Do you have a receipt?"

I didn't have the receipt with me but pointed out that the ventilated pair was priced a bit less and I'd be willing to do an even exchange.

"Now, wait a minute, you don't have a receipt?" Again I said no.

"Well," he remarked, "those could have fallen off a turnip truck."

"No," I chuckled. "A glove truck, maybe, but not a turnip truck. What you're implying is that I might have stolen these gloves or at least didn't buy them here."

"Well, that could have happened."

I told him I didn't think his approach was a very good way to cultivate my future business but suggested we focus on the gloves for the time being. I just wanted to exchange the gloves.

He told me, "These are already opened, they're out of the package, and we can't do the exchange." I asked if he could make an exception to the rules, and he said no.

I said, "Let me talk to your boss, please." So his boss came over and asked, "What's the problem?"

"I want to exchange these gloves."

"Do you have your receipt?"

For the third time, I said, "No, I don't."

"Well, I can't help you."

"Look," I instructed him, "the gloves are unharmed, they're not even dirty. I'm willing to exchange them for the others, an even trade, no refund, and all I want is the other pair of gloves."

"Put yourself in my position," he countered. "If you were in my position, would you feel that you could in good conscience resell those gloves as new?"

"Absolutely. The gloves were never used. They merely spent the night at my house. Now put yourself in my position. Let's not look at just how the exchange should take place, let's look at why we're doing this." (Focus on the purpose rather than the process.)

"You're obviously selling gloves in order to turn a profit," I continued. "You're trying to turn a profit in order to perpetuate your business. And the way you perpetuate your business is by getting not just a glove transaction out of a customer but all of his or her business. This is a motorcycle dealership, and you're selling accessories, parts, and motorcycles.

"I bought my last motorcycle here, and I may buy my next motorcycle here. I pay to have my motorcycle serviced here, and I usually buy my accessories and parts here. I'm worth tens of thousands of dollars to your organization in past and future business. In light of the fact that I'm at least a thirty- to forty-thousand-dollar asset for your company, does it make sense to quibble over an even trade on some twenty-two-dollar gloves?"

He said, "You're right. Take the gloves, and have a great day."

The minute he saw me as the asset I was to his business and stopped thinking of blind adherence to the processes, he treated me like a customer. He also increased the likelihood of getting my future business. Think of the why, and the how will become obvious.

The first factor in our equation was awareness, how you think. The second factor is what you do, the performance aspect.

To bring about your future growth, I propose that you think

about doing more. "Doing more?" you may reply. "There aren't enough hours in the day already! Jim, are you nuts?" No, I'm not. Let me explain. Simply put, we do not grow unless we stretch.

Several years ago, I was asked how to go about getting a raise. I said, "If you want a raise, first give your employer and your customers a raise in your performance; do more than you're required to do. Then they'll have a reason to give you a raise." Radio personality and all-around wise man Earl Nightingale is famous for the story about a woman who was standing in front of a wood-burning stove saying, "Give me heat and then I'll put in the wood." Sometimes we think that just because we are where we are we should be rewarded.

Well, personal growth doesn't work that way. I propose that we should always give more than expected.

Dr. Kenneth McFarland, a well-known motivational speaker back in the seventies and eighties, said, "There are no traffic jams in the extra mile." Going the extra mile always is rare territory.

I believe that maturity is the ability to get yourself to do what needs to be done, when it needs to be done, even when you're not in the mood to do it—and still do it well. What's more, the more mature a person is, the more likely he or she is to do things before they *have to* be done. Another way of saying this is that the person who is a master of his or her craft will tend to do what's required long before it's required.

In any situation, if you just ask, "What is required? Now, what else can I do?" and you add that extra little touch, then you will be programming yourself to stretch, to grow, to find new alternatives. Then you can make a difference. And your difference can help the world start getting better. If all of us did only just what was required, the status quo would exist forever, things would never change. Nothing grows until somebody does more than he or she is paid to do, more than he or she is required to do.

At the beginning, I said there was a formula: high awareness times high performance equals mastery. So let's look at what I mean by high awareness and high performance.

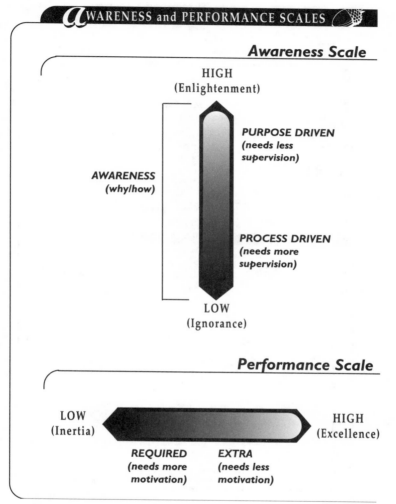

AWARENESS and PERFORMANCE SCALES

Awareness Scale

HIGH
(Enlightenment)

AWARENESS
(why/how)

PURPOSE DRIVEN
*(needs less
supervision)*

PROCESS DRIVEN
*(needs more
supervision)*

LOW
(Ignorance)

Performance Scale

LOW
(Inertia)

HIGH
(Excellence)

REQUIRED
*(needs more
motivation)*

EXTRA
*(needs less
motivation)*

The vertical axis is awareness, which is measured by knowing the purposes and principles, the why of things. More than that, it involves raising your level of thinking in any situation, the ability to get more information or think about the bigger picture. This scale ranges from complete ignorance, not knowing anything, at the bottom, to total enlightenment, knowing everything, at the top.

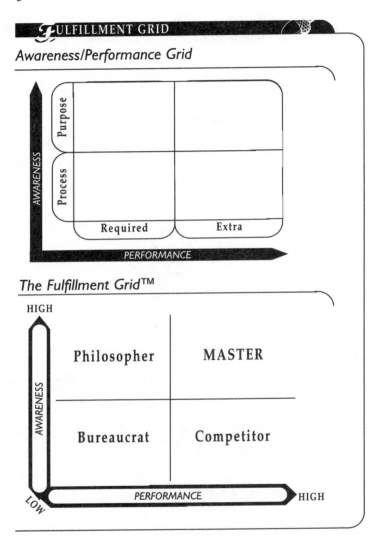

The horizontal axis, performance, ranges from doing nothing at the far left to world-changing behavior on the far right. On the left, we are simply doing the job and no more, doing only what is required. On the right is high performance, doing more than is required, overfilling your space, stretching yourself, growing, contributing a little bit more.

In this model the resulting four quadrants help us identify four modes of operating. We all find ourselves in each of these four modes at one time or another in all categories of our life.

If you are low in awareness and low in performance, then you fit into the lower left quadrant. In the fulfillment grid, I call that section the bureaucrat.

A bureaucrat, in this sense, is someone who does things without question. If you asked a bureaucrat, "Why do you do that?" the answer would be, "It's my job. It has to be done. Somebody's got to do it. And besides, that's how I was told to do it."

Since they are not very self-aware, bureaucrats constantly need to be motivated by someone else. However, as they move forward on the performance scale, their operating mode will change. If they're regularly getting outside of their comfort zone, they'll start to stretch, grow, and do more than is required. They'll need less motivation and simply need to be empowered with good information, the right kind of tools, and the situation where they can control the outcome as much as possible.

In my research I've found that people in the bureaucrat mode don't seem to think very deeply. Rarely do they understand their own Acorn Profile, nor do they see the uniqueness in others. So they tend to be highly judgmental. They don't have the energy or motivation to question the process or authority. And they tend to be confused much of the time. They are passive, waiting for orders or permission. They rarely feel confident enough to take a leadership role. They tend to think as victims.

If someone wants to get out of this bureaucrat mode, how can he do it? He can start asking more questions, start expanding his awareness. Like a three-year-old, he should ask why to everything! As we progress up that awareness scale, we become more and more enlightened and worth more to our organization or to the relationship we're in.

Up the awareness scale, in the upper left quadrant, is the philosopher.

The philosopher mode also does only what's required but thinks about it a lot more. She's figured it out, she understands some of the reasons. A lot of times she slips into the mode of being merely a spectator, a backseat driver. She sits in the stands at the stadium and calls out the instructions that she thinks are right to the people on the field, and of course none of the people on the field hears what she's saying or cares.

Philosophers may know themselves very well, but they take no action to grow. If all we do is become more enlightened, but it doesn't spill over to affect our behavior, we end up being an armchair quarterback in a very lonely situation.

Most philosophers (in this model) tend to become cynical and skeptical, and they tend to become what my fellow speaker Brian Tracy calls an "articulate incompetent." They talk a great game but seldom play in it.

What does a philosopher need to do to move into the realm of mastery? A philosopher needs to do more than is required, such as not just doing your work but actually solving the problem. Putting in whatever effort is necessary to achieve the needed outcome. This could also apply to simple social situations: cleaning up your room when you are a guest in someone's home, or leaving a borrowed car with a full tank of gas when it's returned, or going the extra mile for a neighbor, customer, or employer.

When you start to increase your performance but not your awareness, then you move into the lower right quadrant, which is the competitor.

Competitors tend to be workaholics. It's as if they're running on a treadmill trying to win a race that doesn't exist. They keep turning the speed up, thinking that somewhere in the distance they're going to win. Well, it's not going to happen; all they will get is calluses on their feet! So they're in danger of burnout; they're operating from fear. They're afraid that they're not going to be first or most or best or biggest. They're constantly looking over their shoulders, watching other people to see where they stand in relation to them. In a word, they're *competing*.

And that's a hypertense, uncomfortable way to live because there's no satisfaction in it, no fulfillment. There is a little momentary win, "Yes! I was number one," and then a moment later, "I've got to get back on that treadmill again."

When Will You Know You've Won?

One evening I was in the fitness room at a hotel and struck up a conversation with a fellow traveler. This guy began to tell me about his life, but as he talked it sounded more like a scoreboard. He described his custom-built home in the best section of town, including the detailed history of his antique furniture and the exclusiveness of the imported marble. He regaled me with the importance of his position (with a nationally recognized firm, of course). He told me about his wife's position with her company and the Ivy League colleges they both had graduated from. He listed the accomplishments of his children, including their SAT scores. He even described the pedigree of his dog!

Finally he paused, and I asked, "When will you know you've won?"

He looked at me with a baffled expression, then proceeded to tell me about his new luxury sports car. Obviously, he didn't get it, but I was serious with my question. It was apparent that he spent his life surrounding himself with symbols of success. It was also clear that in the stark environment of a workout room, he was stripped of his "success armor" and needed verbally to re-create it for me, a total stranger.

When we haven't achieved the inner peace that comes from fulfillment, we keep trying to fill the hole within us with "things." It's an impossible, frustrating task just like the mythical Sisyphus who was sentenced eternally to rolling a boulder up a mountain only to have it roll back down.

T H O U G H T   B R E A K
When will you know *you've* won?

If a person will simply improve his or her performance while staying focused on the goal and purpose, he or she will attain a new level of mastery. That's when we enter the quadrant in the upper right-hand corner, the master. That's where life becomes fulfilling.

Masters are contributors; they make a difference in the world and experience a sense of personal fulfillment. Life matters to them, and they feel great about the changes they bring about.

To my way of thinking, the master quadrant is the only mode in which you will find a person achieving fulfillment. Personal fulfillment begins the minute you start doing more than you have to do and the minute you start focusing on why you're doing it.

If you're purpose driven and you're exceeding the requirements, you respect yourself more. Many years ago, the movie *Stand and Deliver* was built around the achievements of Jaime Escalante, one of the great educators in our nation who taught a group of inner-city kids calculus and had them winning awards for doing so. The way he did it was through creative teaching techniques to convey the fundamental principles. And once a person learns the fundamental principles, then he or she can easily figure out the processes. Escalante taught them to attain mastery.

So the upper right quadrant of high awareness and high performance is mastery. As I said before, at this level you're purpose driven, you're exceeding requirements, you're making a difference. Because of this you're also a leader, whether or not your position shows it. Others will naturally follow your lead.

To have more, give more. To know more, notice more. People who do this have a natural glow about them, and other people want to be around them because they're charismatic and magnetic.

It's like when Babe Ruth stepped to the plate and pointed to left field where he was about to hit a home run—and then he did it. Or when General Norman Schwarzkopf briefed the press on how he had orchestrated Operation Desert Storm and won not only our admiration but our affection as well. Or when John F. Kennedy announced boldly that we would put a man on the moon and return him safely to earth in one decade.

These masters clearly had an appeal that defied definition. They knew how and why they were doing what they were doing, and they did much more than they were required to do in at least one area of their life. You can have that, too, whenever you operate from the position of mastery.

Much of this book has led you through the process of increasing your awareness of yourself. But those who are only self-aware aren't fully in the game. Without also mastering the art of self-motivation, your situation never improves. When you can both understand and motivate yourself, then you leave the bureaucrat mode and graduate into the mode of mastery: purpose driven with high performance, a perfect formula for fulfillment.

16. The Future You See
Defines the Person You'll Be

In 1979, Tim Seward sat in my audience wide-eyed and eager to grow. His newly bought Tidy Car franchise provided him the chance to build his own business doing auto detailing. At nineteen years old, this was quite a challenge. He had no college degree or business experience, just enthusiasm and the willingness to work hard.

I spoke to the group on "How to Build Your New Business," and after my speech Tim sat with me during lunch. I tried to answer his scores of questions and still eat lunch. At the end of lunch he asked me for a "daily motivator," a challenging quote to motivate himself with.

Here's what I told him: "Every day ask yourself, 'How would the person I'd like to be do the things I'm about to do?'" He went home and did just that.

His goal was to become the international sales leader of Tidy Car. He wanted to be the best they had. So he asked himself, "How would the international sales leader do what I'm about to do?"

He began to dress differently for work—in a jumpsuit with "Tidy Car" on the back, rather than a T-shirt and jeans. He also did his work more thoroughly. Each car was polished to perfection. He served his customers like the leader would. They came back for more and referred their friends to Tim.

Tim's business rapidly grew, so he leased an old service station and hired others to help. He upgraded all that he did.

Tim listened to motivational and business tapes as he worked.

He went to seminars. He traded auto services for advice and coaching. His business continued to grow.

At the end of that year, Tim had done so well that he won the international sales leader award among hundreds of other franchisees at Tidy Car's convention in New Orleans. He drove home in his prize, a brand-new, shiny white Corvette!

Tim went on to lead Tidy Car again and again. Then he formed his own company selling auto accessories. He became a good husband and father. He learned how to build and sustain a successful business. Today, two decades later, he lives in a beautiful new home in Florida, has built, owned, and sold four business locations in Michigan that provide jobs for many people and produce over six million dollars a year, lives an abundant life, and has a beautiful family!

Tim did not ride a wave of automotive opportunity. Nor did he luck into a business relationship with a rich benefactor. No wise guru took him under his or her wing. He didn't gamble big and win.

He simply practiced what my friend Tony Alessandra, Ph.D., calls "the Platinum Rule." That is, he treated people the way they wanted to be treated. He served them graciously, gave their cars the extra touch, made it easy for them to work with him, valued his coworkers, and constantly increased his own ability to bring value to others.

Tim was rewarded for his work on all levels: good health, great friendships, happy family, successful business . . . abundant life. Not because of college degrees, negotiating skills, financial mastery, or good timing. He was rewarded, as nature always rewards us, by the natural, predictable results of becoming the kind of person he was capable of becoming in all eight areas of his life. He was in alignment with his velocity, his values, his smarts, his bandwidth, and his behavioral style. Naturally, his growth seemed almost automatic. (He was going to become an oak anyway!)

As you apply the Acorn Principle in your life, you, too, will live more abundantly. As you "nurture your nature," the results you seek will come to you. The person you become will attract the relationships and opportunities you desire. Possibilities will arise that you could never have predicted. Great moments will occur as if you, personally, had been singled out by God for a special blessing. When you dedicate yourself to the ongoing process of personal growth, good things will happen in ways that will amaze you.

Success is not a contest, nor is it a mountain you must struggle to climb. Success is your birthright. It is your natural state of being.

Sure, you'll have to work at it. You may even have to develop some new habits. But personal growth (the natural process that creates a successful life) is not drudgery. It is fun! Ask anyone who is living a highly productive and happy life, "What is it like to develop new abilities and bring out your best?" He or she will pause, then smile and tell you, "It is great! I can't imagine living any other way!"

I know this to be true. Over the past twenty-plus years of involvement in human development I have found that the people at the top of every field have a different way of looking at life from those who are still struggling to keep up. It is not a difference in talent. It is a difference in outlook.

How do I know? Because I've seen it happen to Tim Seward and in the lives of thousands of others. I've experienced it in my own life again and again.

Now it's your turn to *NURTURE YOUR NATURE.*

As you take the next Thought Break, take the time to write your answers and date each entry. Keep a journal of these desires and add to it as you read this book, and beyond. Notice how this picture of the future you evolves over the years and how it also stays the same in many ways. The clearer your description of the person you'd like to be, the more likely it is that you'll live the life you'd like to see. Caution: Don't take this exercise lightly. This can be one of the most profound exercises you will ever complete. It establishes a baseline and a target for the application of the rest of the ideas in this book.

THOUGHT BREAK
- What words would best describe the person you'd truly like to be?
- What character traits would you like others to see in you?
- What subjects would you like to know much more about?
- What skills would you like to acquire?
- How would you like to be regarded by others?
- In what places or groups would you like to be accepted and feel comfortable?
- What life experiences would you like to have?
- What credentials would you like to acquire?
- What would you like to do for the world?
- How would the person you'd like to be do what you are about to do?

Once you have described the person you'd like to be, look over your personal priority wheel to see which areas you should be placing more emphasis on today in order to make your dreams a reality.

I truly believe that at any given time, one needs, like a tree, to be either expanding your roots (gaining more awareness and resources) or bearing fruit (behaving productively) in order to grow. When you spend too much time in one area, your needs will increase in the other areas. You need to have a daily plan for both expanding your roots and bearing fruit.

The Thought Diet: Your Growth Starter

The desire to expand my roots and to bear fruit in my life developed into a tool that I've used off and on for more than twenty years. I call it the thought diet. It's designed to influence your thinking through your behavior and to groom your behavior through your thinking. I believe we should take ourselves to raise. And when you're raising someone, there are two jobs, both with the same goal: Both the parent and the child want the child to become an independent, self-directed adult.

If both want independence, how do you get there? Each person must do the appropriate job. For example, it's the child's job to form the right habits that will serve her well in life, keep her safe, and get her goals achieved. It's the parents' role to guide the child's growth and help her select the right habits.

I told my son years ago, "I want the same thing you want. I want you to be able to do whatever you want to do without ever checking with me on whether you can do it or not."

He said, "Hey, I like that."

"Here's how you get there," I told him. "You form the kind of habits—study habits, interpersonal habits, habits in school, habits in daily hygiene, habits in decision making—that will assure me that you're going to make good choices and keep yourself safe as you progress in life. As I see those habits develop in you, I'll give you more and more freedom in every area. So you form the habits, and I'll guide your growth."

Using that thinking, you and I can follow the thought diet to guide our own growth as we develop and cultivate the habits of success. Here's how it works: The thought diet is a tool for helping you become more of the person you need to be in order to achieve your goals. If you cultivate the thoughts and habits of the person you want to be, you'll automatically start getting all the things you want to get. There are four simple rules in this order of importance:

1. Read your thought diet card once every morning and once every night.
2. Limit your contact with cynical or negative people.
3. Perform an unselfish act every day without expecting gratitude.
4. Reread rule number one: Read your thought diet card once every morning and once every night.

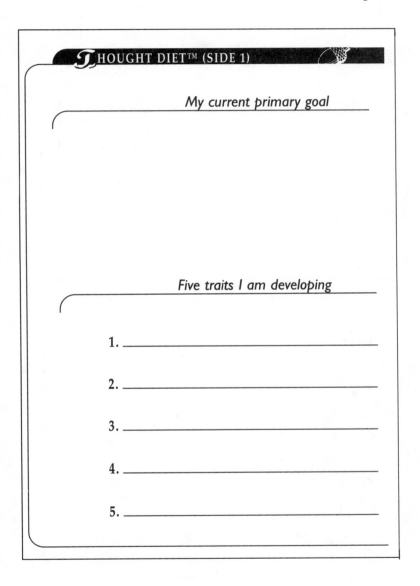

THOUGHT DIET™ (SIDE 1)

My current primary goal

Five traits I am developing

1. _____

2. _____

3. _____

4. _____

5. _____

THOUGHT DIET (SIDE 2)

Minimum Daily Actions

Mind

Body

Spirit

Emotions

Friends

Family

Career

Finances

©1977, ©1997 Jim Cathcart, La Jolla, CA

The thought diet card has three important parts: your current primary goal (a brief description of the goal that matters most in your life right now), traits you are developing (five qualities you most want to cultivate within yourself to become the person you want to be), and minimum daily actions (behaviors that will break your inertia each day and get you started growing again). This is not a mere list of goals to achieve or studies to complete, it is a list of traits and behaviors that bring out the desired qualities in you.

The goal and the list of five traits go on one side of your card, and minimum daily actions go on the other side. On the side of the card for actions, list eight categories: mind, body, spirit, emotions, friends, family, career, and finances. And then beside each one write a minimum action that will help you to grow in that area.

Be realistic here; don't challenge yourself too much or too little. Aim to stay in your zone of optimal velocity. Here's what my card looked like in 1975.

- "My current primary goal" was to become a *national expert in the field of personal development.*
- "Five traits I am developing" were
  1. to be more *observant:* to notice more, and to learn from every source available
  2. to be *healthy, fit,* and *agile:* constantly to develop physically
  3. to be *generous:* to compliment others often, to help them find the good in themselves
  4. to be *optimistic:* always to look for solutions and possibilities
  5. to be *inspiring:* to hold myself to a higher set of professional and personal standards
- For my "Minimum Daily Actions," I wanted to take actions in each of those eight categories that would cause me to develop the five traits on the other side of the card.

The Future You See Defines the Person You Need to Be

I knew that if I developed the traits I would start becoming the person who would achieve the goal I had written down. Then the goal would be the natural by-product of the daily actions. It's kind of the reverse of what a lot of people do, which is to focus solely on the goal. But I say you can go about it from either direction. If you figure out what kind of person you want to be, then think about the goals that person would achieve, and then become the person—the goals will be the automatic by-product.

Here's what was on my Minimum Daily Actions side of the card. For my *mind,* I wrote: *Every day without fail, I will read one page of a book.* My goal for a minimum daily action was not to feed my mind an enormous quantity of information all at once; it was just to make sure that every single day I did something to improve my mind. So I identified several books to read. I even had a few paperback books that I'd tear one page out of and carry with me to be sure that I would read it. After a while I became more disciplined in that area and raised my goals. By starting with reading only one page of a book every day I developed the discipline to read several pages a day and ultimately read ten times what I used to.

For my *body,* to enhance my health I knew that I needed to jog more often. But rather than commit to jogging every day, which I knew was not likely to happen, I put down a goal that may seem silly to you but it worked for me. I wrote: *Every day I'll put on my jogging shoes and walk out to the street.* That's it, and some days that is literally all I did: I put on my jogging shoes, walked out to the street, came back in the house, took them off, and sat down to have dinner. But by forcing myself every day to put the shoes on and walk to the street, I increased the likelihood of my going for a jog by a hundredfold, and I ended up getting in good physical shape for the first time in my adult life. The toughest part of any fitness program is to get yourself to show up regularly ready to exercise.

Under the area of *spirit,* I wrote a simple goal: *Thank God every day for the blessings I have received.* I wanted to take some time every day to pause and reflect on my blessings and to express gratitude. At the end of each day I would say, "Thank you, God, for this good day." Then I'd review the events of the day to find the good in it. I always managed to find something, no matter how small. I still do this today more than twenty years later. And I always find something to be thankful for.

Under *emotions,* I wrote: *I will laugh once today.* Once a day, I would find some excuse, some stimulus, some way to achieve one good belly laugh. This made me conscious of humor all around me and forced me to sustain an openness to laughter. I stopped being so serious all the time, and it made daily living a little more fun.

Under the category of *friends,* I wrote: *I will make a phone call or write to one person I care about today.* In some cases it was a simple little note, and in other cases it was a card or a letter. But this was so much more than I usually did. The result was that I reconnected with some special friends and enriched my life in the process. With E-mail, today I'm even more likely to stay connected with them.

Under the category of *family,* I wrote: *I'll spend ten minutes listening to each member of my family today in one-on-one focused conversation.* In other words, I would pay exclusive attention to that person for at least ten minutes a day. Listening, not telling. The averages nationwide are that most parents spend very little time with their children each day and very little time talking in a meaningful way with each other. By committing to myself I would spend at least ten minutes every day with Paula and with Jim Junior, I increased the quality of communication in our home. Of course, I often spoke with them for a lot longer than ten minutes at a time, but the ten-minute minimum made sure I paid specific attention to them and got the communication started.

Under *career,* I wrote: *I'll learn one new idea today that will enhance my career.* So every day I would look for some way to learn something—anything—either simple or profound. The snowball effect of this was tremendous! Every week I learned at least five new things.

Under *finances,* I wrote: *I will keep an accurate record of the money I received and spent today.* By knowing where the money came from and where it went, I was much more self-directed. As I've often heard, "Things that are measured tend to improve." This habit led to my thinking about my finances more often, and I managed my money better than ever before.

Now, those minimum actions don't constitute a complete plan for becoming a national expert, but they did provide the simple push I needed each day to get started, and it worked for me. I changed the card often, and if I found I wasn't doing something on the card, I would write in a new action, constantly monitoring what I did and what I avoided. I did this repeatedly until I figured out how best to motivate myself and determine what I could get myself to do. If the goal wasn't exciting, then I'd reexamine my goals and put a different goal on the card for a while. If it seemed that I'd acquired one of the five traits, then I'd add some new ones that I felt I needed to work on.

For your own thought diet, don't do exactly as I did. Instead, adapt this tool to your use. But take care to not change the four rules of the thought diet. They are what make the diet work.

Chores: They Are Everywhere in Life

The categories of goal, traits, and minimum actions will keep you on the path toward becoming the person you were naturally designed to be. These actions on the thought diet are your chores, and it is helpful to think of them as daily chores or tasks.

When I was a child, one of my chores at home was to take out the garbage. I knew that if I didn't do my chores for an extended period of time, our house would fill up with garbage. Well, the thought diet steps are *your* chores. When you don't do these chores for an extended period of time, your life fills up with garbage.

> THOUGHT BREAK
> How many of the eight areas of your life have you de-
> veloped today? Where will you keep your thought
> diet card?

The next time you find some unscheduled time, take a moment and do a quick personal priority-wheel assessment. See
which parts of your life are getting your attention. Then use the
thought diet to quickly plan some adjustments. These little
"course corrections" will have an amazing effect on your life.

Don't turn this into work and start to fret over it. Just stop occasionally to notice more of how fully you are living. Then take
some small first steps to live even more.

Review your inner circle every week or two to see whom you
are spending your time with and notice what you are spending
your life on. If you don't like the way you are investing your energies, make some adjustments. Move some outer circle people
into the inner circle and some inner circle people to the outer
circle for a while. These little actions will amaze you with the
value they bring to your life. Profile each person in your inner
circle using the elements of the Acorn Profile. Look for align-
ments and differences between them and you.

Go back to each chapter and review your own notes and un-
derlines. Reassess your velocity, values, intellect, behavioral style,
and more. Read the books in the bibliography to explore each
area further. Call the authors and ask questions. Take personal
initiative to stimulate your growth. Find categories I didn't men-
tion in this book and explore those too. The idea is for you to
continue on a never-ending quest for self-awareness. Never stop
learning more about yourself.

In this book you have traveled a long way from where your
thoughts were before reading it. You've come to notice more
about yourself than 99 percent of people do. This aware-

ness has equipped you to live more fully than ever before. Regardless of job requirements, financial pressures, or family commitments, you have discovered scores of ways to expand your life.

Do it! Don't let these life impulses die in the pages of this book. I wrote these words and did this research so that *you* could live more abundantly.

You've been given a vehicle and an avenue. Your acorn contains unlimited potential for abundant living. This book has sparked many "ahas" of ways to express your life even better. The potential within you is your *vehicle* for making this world a better place. If you don't act on it, all of us miss out. If you do, all of us benefit.

Your relationships and your circumstances are your *avenues* for self-expression. So follow those growth impulses. Tap your potential. The seed of your future successes already lives within and around you. The seed's only job is to grow, to live fully. The oak sleeps within you. Growing season is here.

Nurture your nature!

Afterword

One of the great tragedies of the developed world is limited living. With the freedom to live as we choose, most of us still live less than we could or perhaps should. How little our lives become! While the rest of the world is struggling to find enough food and shelter to survive, we get bored or insecure and shrink our lives to a tiny replica of what they could be.

Are you as fully alive as you'd like to be? I hope so. But I suspect that there is more living available to you. To illustrate where the opportunities are, I offer a description of my own life in recent weeks. It is clearly an example of very high velocity, but it also shows the variety in my life.

As you read, hold me accountable for following my own rules and "walking my talk." See how this description illustrates living fully, balancing one's priorities, aligning with one's natural strengths, and growing the seeds of potential.

In the past forty days I've done so many diverse things that, in retrospect, I don't see how it was all possible within only a six-week period. Without operating in a frenetic or highly stressed way, I've delivered speeches and seminars in nine cities and visited several of my professional speaker and author colleagues.

I've had another birthday, lost a good friend age eighty-nine, given encouragement to a friend who had breast cancer, talked with and E-mailed about thirty other colleagues, and completed the manuscript for this book. I've jogged on the California coast, in Minneapolis, and in Chicago, ridden in a twenty-foot-tall "monster truck" in a rodeo arena, toured Opryland, gone to three plays—*Rent, Forever Plaid,* and *Smokey Joe's Cafe*—had family house guests for a week, attended an art festival, revamped our patio garden, watched a dozen movies, and gone out to eat more than thirty times.

I've read two new books and scores of magazines and newsletters, ridden my motorcycle a dozen times, counseled a depressed friend, romanced my wife, moved out of one office and into another, conducted a national video conference from my office, and organized a new promotional campaign.

I attended a hot rod show in Spokane, walked along a lake in Idaho, watched an IMAX movie, attended an Indian powwow, collaborated with my partner in a software company, sold a handful of learning systems to others who were building their consulting and speaking practices, wrote sympathy cards and personal letters, sent birthday wishes to several people, bought a new life insurance policy, got a massage, got a haircut, rode my motorcycle from San Diego to San Francisco and back with Paula, and visited our son in Santa Barbara.

I accepted the chairmanship of a professional committee and agreed to serve on the board of directors for a nonprofit organization. I spent a morning with a speech coach, began doing voice exercises again, delivered a eulogy for a departed colleague, called my mom twice, met a movie star, went to a "designer's showcase" home, got a chiropractic adjustment, congratulated two friends on their weddings, met with my Japanese publisher at a local hotel restaurant, redesigned one of my business brochures, scheduled a new recording session for an infomercial, reconnected with a treasured old friend, booked several speaking dates, and thanked and praised my staff.

I bought some new clothes, wrote two stories for a *Chicken Soup* book, revamped my Web site, lost my temper, apologized to a colleague I had not stayed in touch with, attended two homeowner association meetings, slept late twice on off days, hired two editors, and reread my manuscript three times. I viewed videotapes of two speeches I had delivered, consulted with two colleagues on their speaking and marketing, studied materials on a dozen of my clients, prepared handouts for future speeches, and bought a new painting for my living room.

I savored a sunset in Squaw Valley and a sunrise in Napa Valley. I watched old movies with good friends and had dinner at the

Lodge at Pebble Beach, lunch on the Big Sur coast, breakfast at Alice's Restaurant, and rode through the Redwood Forest and Sonoma's wine country. I went to a street fair, got stuck in traffic in Oakland, noticed a slight earthquake tremor in Los Angeles, took a course in motorcycle racing on Sears Point Raceway (on my own bike!), sent flowers to Paula for her birthday, and helped her select new dinnerware for our home. I also took out the garbage, laughed with neighbors, emptied some old files, and read lots of mail. All of this took place within one forty-day period.

Now review the above and notice how it touches on the eight areas in the personal priority wheel: mind, body, spirit, emotions, friends, family, career, and finances. As you look, also note that there is room for both inner circle and outer circle relationships as well as new ones. Check to see if time is spent in learning and self-improvement in order to grow.

See if this list is all about me meeting my needs or whether I have made time for the needs of others. Am I getting outside of my zone of optimal velocity or staying mostly within it? Can you tell from these activities ("by their actions you shall know them") what my top three values are? How about my bandwidth? Is there evidence of my top three smarts? What kind of background imprints am I building for tomorrow? Does this description seem to reduce my potential psychological blind spots? Can you tell whether I have a sense of purpose and meaning in my life? My behavioral style is socializer—does the above bear this out? Now imagine that you were investing in me, as if I were a stock. What kind of future growth could you expect based on the foregoing description of my current lifestyle and priorities?

Now apply the same thinking to yourself. Make a thorough list of all that you have done or experienced in the last thirty days. List it all just as I did. The size of your list may surprise you. Then ask the same questions of you that you asked regarding me.

There is so much more living available to you. It may not even require you to do more than you are currently doing. Just doing things differently and being aware might increase your results.

If you are not living abundantly, then get out your thought diet card and start growing. Turn off the TV for a few days and call some friends or family. Get out of the house, talk with your neighbors, volunteer to help some-one, fix something that is broken. Above all, connect with people. Do this in whatever healthy ways will expand your life. The world isn't waiting for you, you have been waiting for it. It is fully operational already. Now make sure you, too, are operating fully. Live your life, don't wait for it.

I am honored that you took the time to read this book. I hope that my words have made a positive impression in your life. If you and I can set the example for others, on any level, life will advance. Thank you for investing part of your life with me.

Further Uses of
The Acorn Principle

There are multiple ways in which this book can be used to expand your life.

Thought Breaks:

Throughout the book these Thought Breaks have been inserted to allow you to explore the ideas presented. Use these as discussion stimulators or as reflection questions to explore yourself more fully. For a complete listing of them visit our Web site at www.cathcart.com.

Discussion Groups:

Groups and couples can use *The Acorn Principle* to get to know each other better than ever before. Review one chapter at a time and compare notes. Discover your internal diversity and gain both self-awareness and the understanding of others.

Relationship Improvement:

Students, teachers, parents and children, couples, family groups, executive teams, employers, employees, coworkers, teams, grandparents, friends, consultants, clients, counselors, doctors, patients, partnerships, people embarking on a new career or life event, problem solving groups, seniors communities, sales people, negotiators, training directors, coaches, talent scouts, interviewers, career counselors, clergy, marriage counselors, and more can benefit from the insights of the Acorn Profile. Use this book for parlor games, salon evenings, discussions, bonding, clarifying agreements, and exploring ways to expand your relationships and your life.

The Acorn Principle was written to enable you to notice more about yourself and find more ways to connect with others. Test its value in all areas of your life. Live fully and grow.

Cathcart Institute

Since 1977 Jim Cathcart has been conducting seminars and delivering exciting speeches on self-awareness and business growth. More than two thousand audiences have heard his compelling presentations in forty-nine states and worldwide from Australia to Europe. With more than twenty years of research and experience in a variety of industries, the depth of information is constantly expanding.

Cathcart Institute offers training in the following areas:
- The Acorn Principle—The Power of Self-Awareness
- Relationship Selling—Growing Business Relationships
- Helping People Grow—Bringing Out the Strengths
- A New Era of Growth— Rethinking Business Relationships

Cathcart Institute clients include almost every imaginable industry. Many of the Fortune 500 companies and leading professional associations use Jim Cathcart's materials in their ongoing training programs. Special custom-designed programs are often created for unique applications.

On-line communities and services are connected via Cathcart Institute's Web site at http://www.cathcart.com. Distance learning and video conferencing are also available.

As past president of the National Speakers Association and recipient of its highest awards for speaking excellence, Jim Cathcart is a leader among professional speakers. His multimedia performances have been popular with convention audiences for two decades.

For further information or to schedule a speaking engagement by Jim Cathcart, contact:

Cathcart Institute
Business Growth Specialists
PO Box 9075
La Jolla, CA 92038-9075
800-222-4883
619-456-3813
Fax: 619-456-7218
E-mail: info@cathcart.com
Web site: www.cathcart.com